50 Ways to Paint Ceilings and Floors

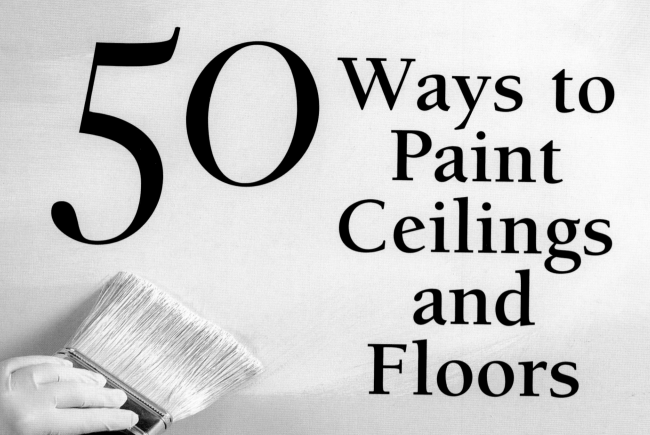

50 Ways to Paint Ceilings and Floors

The Easy
Step-by-Step Way to
Decorator Looks

Elise C. Kinkead

Creative Publishing
international
Minneapolis, Minnesota

This book is dedicated to the spirit of … what if … in us all.

Elise C. Kinkead

Creative Publishing international

Copyright © 2008
Creative Publishing international, Inc.
400 First Avenue North
Suite 300
Minneapolis, Minnesota 55401
1-800-328-3895
www.creativepub.com

Printed in China

10 9 8 7 6 5 4 3 2 1

Library of Congress Cataloging-in-Publication Data

Kinkead, Elise.
  50 ways to paint ceilings and floors : the easy, step-by-step way to
decorator looks / Elise Kinkead.
    p. cm.
ISBN-13: 978-1-58923-365-2 (soft cover)
  ISBN-10: 1-58923-365-4 (soft cover)
  1. House painting--Amateurs' manuals. 2. Texture painting--Amateurs'
manuals. 3. Floors--Amateurs' manuals. 4. Ceilings--Amateurs' manuals.
I. Title. II. Title: Fifty ways to paint ceilings and floors.
TT323.K38 2008
698'.1--dc22   2007052892

President/CEO: Ken Fund
VP for Sales & Marketing: Kevin Hamric

Home Improvement Group

Publisher: Bryan Trandem
Acquisition Editor: Barbara Harold
Managing Editor: Tracy Stanley
Senior Editor: Mark Johanson
Editor: Jennifer Gehlhar

Creative Director: Michele Lanci-Altomare
Senior Design Manager: Brad Springer
Design Managers: Jon Simpson, Sara Holle, James Kegley

Lead Photographer: Steve Galvin
Photo Coordinator: Joanne Wawra
Shop Manager: Bryan McLain
Shop Assistant: Cesar Fernandez Rodriguez

Production Managers: Linda Halls, Laura Hokkanen

Author: Elise C. Kinkead
Cover Design: Laura Shaw
Page Layout Artist: Lois Stanfield
Photographers: Andrea Rugg
Shop Help: David Hartley, Scott Boyd

Contents

50 Ways to Paint Ceilings and Floors

Special CEILINGS

1 Haloed Ceiling

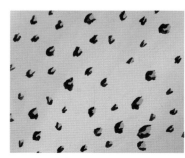

2 Metallic Paint

3 Aluminum Roll Gilding

4 Venetian Plaster

5 Easy Sky

6 Formal Sky

7 Celestial Sky

8 Leopard

9   Stamped Stars

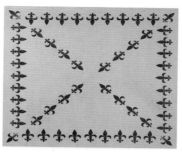

10   Stamped Motifs

11   Faux Drapery

12   Large Graphic

13   Applied Leaf Motifs

14   Elaborate Stencil

15   Decorative Molding

16   Faux Tin Ceiling

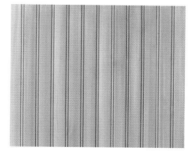

17   Antiqued Embossed Material

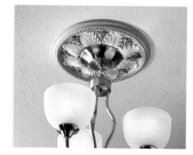

18   Ceiling Medallion

19   Cambric Cloth

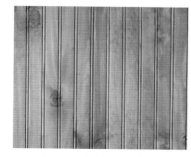

20   Weathered Beadboard

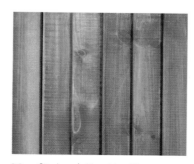

21   Beadboard Stained & Antiqued

22   Stained Knotty Pine

(continued)

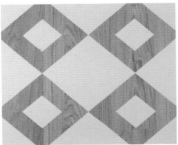

Fantastic FLOORS

23   Floor Cloth

24   Jute Monogram

25   Diamonds on the Floor

26   Bubbles

27   Distressed Painted Hardwood Floor

28   Center Star Medallion

29   Colored Japan Inlay

30   Distressed Fir Floor

31   Decking Multi Paints

32   Decking Semitransparent Stains

33   Faux Bois Repair

34   Antiqued Brick Pavers

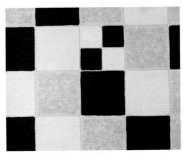

35   Freshened Sheet Vinyl

36   Awning Stripes

37 Arcs & Circles

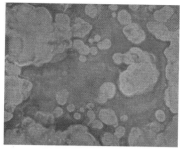

38 Faux Cement Stain

39 French Ironwork Stencil

40 Cement to Stone

41 Bluestone with Brick

42 Venetian Pavers

And So
Much
MORE

43 Faux Bois Door

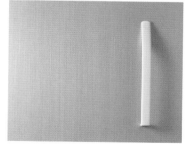

44 Faux Stainless Steel

45 Frosted Mirror

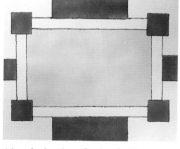

46 Imitation Stained Glass

47 Antiqued Crown Molding

48 Aged Molding

49 Metallic Tiles

50 Reverse Color Molding

Introduction

CEILINGS AND FLOORS are the largest surface areas found in a room and the least paid attention to!

It is time to pay attention to these areas. *50 Ways to Paint Ceilings and Floors* demonstrates many different techniques that will allow some justice to be brought to the oftentimes overlooked yet wonderful blank canvases that a ceiling and a floor can be.

The "More" demonstrations are intended to round off the repertoire of painted techniques of some other commonly overlooked surfaces that are indeed integral to the overall look and feel of a room.

Doors, windows, woodwork, and yes, even the refrigerator, can all become part of the design scheme.

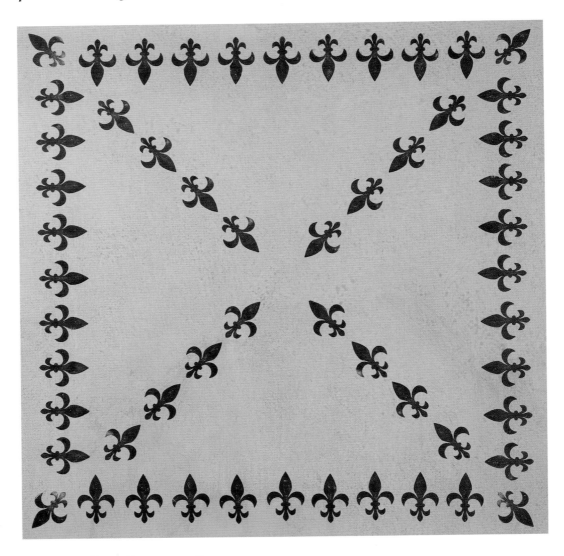

Do not be shy about painting your ceiling or floor with any one of these techniques; keep in mind it is only paint. When a ceiling is painted with one of the simple techniques found in this book or merely painted in a wonderful and maybe even an unexpected color, the ceiling becomes a wonderful "lid," the finishing touch that caps off your entire room, a room that you have worked very hard on making beautiful.

Painting a floor likewise supports the overall design elements of the room and it is truly wonderful to discover that a floor has been asked to take part in the room's design. Imagine bubbles peeking out from underneath a plain or fanciful rug.

Painting floors can be a wonderfully inexpensive way to nudge that floor into a few more years of service and allows for your unique creative expression to take place.

Whenever you set forth to apply a painted finish, do so with confidence, wonder, and enjoyment and your work will look beautiful.

The demonstrations you find here are meant to employ and rely upon the philosophy of "The Economy of The Artist," which simply means: use the most efficient number of steps to arrive at your intended result. This concept is one that should be applied when painting the large surfaces of ceilings and floors; after all, painting these areas does take a bit of physical exertion due to their size and you really do not need to spend any more time than necessary to accomplish your creation.

Did you know that keeping your arms extended above your head for 20 minutes is equal to 1 hour of cardiovascular aerobic exercise? It is according to some, so you will also be getting the benefits of a great workout!

Enjoy the journey into the lesser-known areas of painting ceilings, floors, and more!

TIP FROM THE AUTHOR

Step Zero

Every time an artist, a craftsperson, or a do-it-yourselfer starts a project, the aim is the same: SUCCESS. There is a secret to achieving that—always start at Step Zero.

Starting at Step Zero means reading all pertinent introductory sections and then reading through the project instructions before starting to paint. *50 Ways to Paint Ceilings and Floors* suggests you buy high-quality equipment for the best project outcome. Being fully prepared by equipping yourself with knowledge and proper tools and materials helps you create the great finish you want.

Basics

Ceiling prep is very much like wall prep. If there are areas that are cracked or have holes, follow these helpful steps.

Fixing Common Problems

Water Stains

Problem: Unsightly water or rust stains require immediate attention because they may indicate a leak somewhere.

Solution: Check for leaking pipes or damaged flashing on the roof. Before you paint, repair the leak. If the surface is soft or crumbling, repair the area. To seal and cover a water-stained area that is not otherwise damaged, use a stain-sealing primer that contains shellac. If left unsealed, the stain will eventually show through your new paint job.

Colored Stains

Problem: Black marks and other stains like crayon or marker are not always easily removed.

Solution: Apply a stain remover to a clean, dry cloth and rub lightly on the stain. Cover any stain that is not completely removed with a stain-sealing primer that contains shellac.

Mildew and Mold

Problem: Because mold and mildew grow in damp areas, check kitchen and bathroom surfaces carefully.

Solution: Test the stain by washing it with water and detergent. If it is mildew, it will not wash away. Wash the area with a solution of one part chlorine bleach to four parts water, which will kill the mildew spores. Scrub with a soft-bristle brush. Then wash the mildew away with a TSP solution, rinse with clear water, and allow the area to dry thoroughly before painting.

Peeling Paint

Problem: Peeling paint occurs for a number of reasons and it must be removed before you repaint.

Solution: Scrape away the loose paint with a putty knife or paint scraper. Apply a thin coat of spackle to the edges of the chipped paint, using a putty knife. Allow it to dry. Sand the area with 150-grit sandpaper, creating a smooth transition between bare ceiling and surrounding painted surfaces. Wipe clean with a damp sponge. Spot-prime the area with polyvinyl acrylic (PVA) primer.

Filling Small Nail Holes

1. Using a putty knife or your finger, force a small amount of drywall compound or spackle into the hole, filling it completely. Scrape the area smooth with the putty knife and let dry.

2. Sand the area lightly with 150-grit sandpaper. Wipe clean with a damp sponge, let dry, and dab on PVA primer.

Fixing Popped Drywall Nails

Drywall nails can work themselves loose, either popping through the drywall or creating a small bulge on the surface.

1. Drive a new wallboard screw into place 2" (5 cm) below the popped nail, sinking the head slightly below the wall surface. Be sure

the screw hits the stud and pulls the drywall tight against the framing, taking care not to damage the ceiling surface.

2. Scrape away loose paint or drywall material around the popped nail. Drive the popped nail back into the framing, sinking the head slightly below the drywall surface.

3. Using a drywall knife, cover both the nail hole and the new screw hole with spackle. Sand and prime the patched areas.

Filling Dents and Gouges in Drywall

1. Scrape away any drywall paper, using a drywall knife, if necessary. Sand the dented or gouged area lightly. Using a drywall knife, fill the dent or hole with spackle. For deep holes or dents, build up the spackle in layers, allowing each layer to dry before adding another.

2. Sand the patched area with fine-grit sandpaper; seal the area with PVA primer.

Patching Holes in Drywall

1. For a larger problem, cut a neat rectangle around the hole, using a drywall saw. Cut backer strips from drywall or wood; insert them into the opening and hot-glue them to the back of the opening.

2. Cut a rectangular drywall patch slightly smaller than the opening; secure it in place to the backing strips, using hot glue.

3. Apply self-adhesive drywall tape over the cracks, then spackle. After drying, sand the area smooth and apply PVA primer.

4. Self-adhering fiberglass and metal repair patches are available for quick and easy repairs. Simply apply the patch over the hole. Then coat the area with spackle, blending into the surrounding wall. After drying, sand it smooth and apply primer.

All About Paint

A good basecoat of paint is extremely important to any of the techniques demonstrated in this book. Never use "ceiling white" or "ceiling" paint because the paint is just too absorbent and this will cause you trouble when attempting any of the outlined techniques.

A quick way to check to see if your ceiling paint is too absorbent is to take a wet rag and wipe it on your ceiling; if the water soaks in within 30 seconds, you should apply a proper coat of paint.

Use a high-quality latex or acrylic paint, just as you would for your walls.

50 Ways to Paint Ceilings and Floors includes painting on just about any type of flooring material.

There are as many opinions as there are painters when it comes to the best way and with what to paint these surfaces. The best advice to follow is that of a trusted clerk at your local paint store. New products are coming on the market as we speak and the clerk will be up to date on these new products.

Please be aware that companies are coming up with wonderful water-based products every day and most of the demonstrations shown in this book will use water-based products, except in a few cases. However, all the demonstrations in this book can be done with a water-based product if you just take your time and are patient with yourself.

When preparing most floor surfaces you will want to clean any dirt, grease, and wax from the surface.

Depending on what you are painting on the floor, you may be directed to apply a primer. Keep in mind that today some of the best primers are water-based.

A good primer should seal the surface below it and create a firm bonding film for subsequent layers of paint to follow; this is why you do not want to omit a primer coat if one is called for.

Flooring paints today have made vast improvements in terms of color and durability and I cannot stress enough that some of the best products to use are the water-based variety, which are also better for you and the environment.

The question always comes up if a water-based polyurethane can be applied over oil-based stains. The answer is, yes, as long as the oil-based stain has had time to completely dry, which could take up to 30-plus days depending on temperature and humidity.

For topcoats choose either a water-based polyurethane or an oil-based polyurethane. Always use the right tools for the right job. The photos show the appropriate applicators for water-based and oil-based polyurethanes.

Applicator Oil

Applicator Water

Specialty paints for masonry and decking are also available and yes, these too come in water-based formulas and are quite good.

You will be surprised at the availability of the right paint for your job.

Okay, you have decided to paint your ceiling, but it has "popcorn" texture all over it. What to do?

Remove it.

If you are lucky, the texture has not been painted, in which case you can do one of two things:

Scrape it down with a stiff 6" (15.2 cm) drywall blade. This will not remove everything, but will "knock down" the pebbly bumps to an acceptable finish. The semi-roughness can even be a positive aesthetic element on your ceiling.

Always wear protective eyewear.

Before any painting takes place you will need to prime the texture material; do so with latex-based primer.

If the texture is of a certain make-up, you may get very lucky and be able to simply take a wet wallpaper sponge and smooth the texture down to an almost perfect finish.

Always wear protective eyewear.

Important Safety Precaution Regarding Popcorn Texture and Asbestos

If your ceiling was applied prior to 1979, there is a very good likelihood that the material contains asbestos. You can buy a test kit at your local paint store to check for asbestos. Discuss the test kit and procedure with your paint store clerk. DO NOT scrape any ceiling texture until you carefully read and understand all of the directions. If your texture does contain asbestos, it is best to hire a company that specializes in the removal of asbestos.

Always have the color of your primer tinted the same or very close to the color of your finish paint. This will make your job much easier and if you are a good painter, you will only need to apply one primer coat and one finish coat.

Painting Techniques

Universal Tinting Colorant (UTC)

UTC is not paint, but an additive used to tint all types of paint. In fact, it's used in the machine at the paint store to color paint. UTC comes in small tubes or pint sizes; buy the smallest tube, as it is a very powerful color agent. In addition to tinting paint, it also tints varnishes. UTCs never dry on their own, so wipe up spills quickly or the UTC will spread over everything. UTCs are transparent until added to paint.

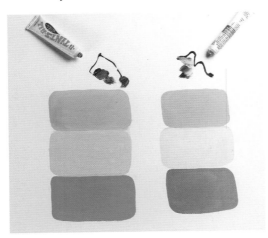

Blending

After applying a coat of oil-based or water-based paint, but before it sets up, use an off-loaded brush to gently brush in a crosshatch pattern over the top of the paint. This softly blends paint and knocks down paintbrush ridges.

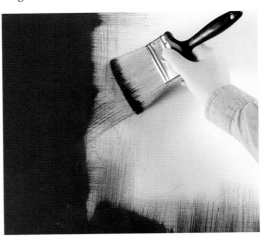

French Brush

This technique spreads the paint over the surface quickly with total coverage. Apply the paint in a crisscross fashion, arcing in and around and ending with an upstroke off the surface. Use either a straight or angled-edge paintbrush.

Pouncing

Apply glaze or paint using the French brush technique and while it's wet, tap perpendicularly on the surface with a 2" (5.1 cm) oval sash paintbrush using moderate pressure. This technique gives you a very tight "dotted" surface. The end result should look even, but a slight variation here and there is okay. This is a good way to blend two colors together.

Folding

To fold a glaze means to soften the texture and to reduce contrast and pattern, usually by lightly patting the surface with a pad of 90-weight cheesecloth.

Using Cheesecloth

The example shown below is the appropriate shape of a 90-weight cheesecloth pad. The side that touches the paint surface is fairly smooth, without wrinkles or little tails.

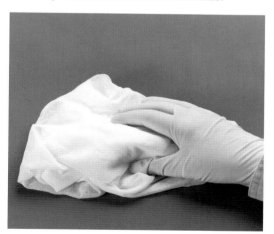

Caulking

It is always a more beautiful paint job if you take a minute to caulk along moldings and trim after priming and before applying the finish coat of paint. Run a bead of paintable caulk, dip your finger in some water, and smooth the caulk out with your wet finger.

Traditionally, natural woodwork is not caulked; only caulk a painted surface to a painted surface.

Pulling Tape

Always pull the tape away from the freshly painted surface at a 45° angle. If the fresh paint is wet, this will ensure that you do not pull the tape across the fresh paint; if the fresh paint is dry, this will put less "stress" on the paint.

Wet Edge

To keep a wet edge means that the outside section of the applied paint is not allowed to dry. Thus, when applying more paint, you may work wet paint into wet paint, which will create a smoother paint surface.

All About Stains

Use stains to add color to wood. There are many colors and types, and compatible types may be mixed to make custom colors. Whatever type of stain you choose, wipe it on with one lint-free T-shirt rag and wipe it off with a clean one.

Gel Stain

Full-bodied gel stains are easy to work with and can be used as an overglaze right from the can. Find them in paint stores. In the top example, a red mahogany was applied over birch wood.

Pure Color Stain

Water-based liquid and very concentrated dry powder dyes are used to stain wood and are available in water-based liquid concentrate and dry powder concentrated dyes that are mixed with water. These pure color stains are used to add vivid color to raw wood. You may mix liquid concentrate stain with liquid concentrate stain; likewise you may mix dry powder dye with dry powder dye to create custom coloration.

Japan Color

Japan Color is a super finely ground oil-based pigment. Mix the Japan Color to a skim milk consistency with mineral spirits, wipe on, and immediately wipe off.

The Japan Paint palette is very beautiful and extensive and given that this is paint, it can easily be used over any type of paint or varnish.

Safety Procedures

Always wear safety glasses, dust masks, and gloves as necessary to protect yourself when sanding and working with paints and solvents. Always read manufacturer's instructions for proper cleanup and disposal information. Always work in well-ventilated areas to avoid build-up of fumes.

Safety Caution

If you are using any stain that is not water-based, the rags used for staining are combustible. Linseed oil (found in most staining materials) causes them to give off heat as they dry, enabling them to self-combust. Never throw a dirty staining rag in your trash. Fill an empty gallon-size paint container with water. When finished staining, immerse the rags in the water and tightly seal the lids. Dispose of the materials properly.

All About Moldings

There are many ways to paint a molding. The most common technique is to slightly antique the molding so that the carving is enhanced by the antiquing paint being allowed to remain in the crevices while the antiquing paint is lightly removed from the raised portion of the carving.

Antiquing a molding is also a good way to change the color without painting on an entire fresh coat of different colored paint.

The photo top right is a "positive" antiquing method. This simply means that a darker color has been applied over a light base. Notice how much more of the carving you see.

The photo bottom right is a light color over a dark base, which will be referred to as a "negative antiquing" application.

Note that in both photos the light and dark colors are the same, merely reversed. This is a good example of how basecoat can influence color.

All About Color

Put a splash of color into your life and do the unexpected; after all, it is only paint. Even if you decide not to apply any of the ceiling techniques outlined in this book, consider a color for your ceiling along with more interesting woodwork colors. If you do not want to repaint all of your woodwork, at least consider painting the crown molding (if you have it) with your ceiling color.

When the elements of ceilings, walls, and woodwork are considered all together and designed to play off of one another, beautifully stunning and even unexpected harmonies can be achieved within an environment.

Following are a mere three-color palettes to ponder.

Top right: Imagine yellow walls and a coral ceiling all framed by an off-white woodwork color. Reminiscent of a seaside cottage, this palette is versatile and lively. It would be beautiful within a traditional or contemporary setting.

Middle right: Go a little further and deepen the palette for more drama: green walls with a rich golden woodwork color offset by a medium beige ceiling. Richness and luxury will be implied with this handsome palette.

Bottom right: Okay, you do not want that much color? Create a sophisticated monochromatic color palette. Use darker gray for walls and a lighter version of wall color for the ceiling, and tie it all together with an even lighter version for all of the woodwork.

Even a monochromatic approach will create cohesiveness and pull the elements of wall, floor, ceiling, and trim together.

Of course, to complement any color palette, always consider the floor. Any of the floor techniques outlined here would be the final touch to incorporating all the elements of a room together in a harmonious palette of color, texture, and interest.

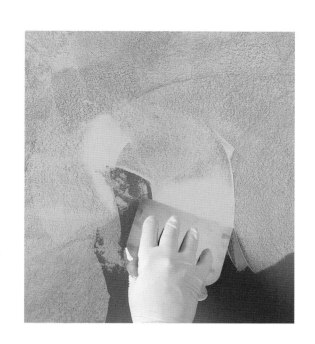

Special
CEILINGS

1 Haloed Ceiling

DON'T WANT TO PAINT your whole ceiling, but do want to give it a nudge toward interesting? Partially paint it.

Applying a soft painted finish to just the perimeter area of a ceiling is referred to as "haloing" the ceiling. This technique will give a softly faded color gradation around the edge of your room and subtly shade the outer edges and corners of the ceiling.

It's a great way to introduce just a blush of color in an otherwise continuous flat, solidly painted ceiling area.

Perfect for traditional homes or contemporary settings.

If for some reason your ceiling is painted in oil-based paint, merely switch the following directions to use oil-based products.

If your ceiling is painted in sheen paint, use the same sheen paint for the haloing paint.

- paint that is the same as existing ceiling paint
- appropriate paint in your color choice to create the halo
- flat latex brush, 4" (10.2 cm)

1 Using the French brush technique of paint application, apply the halo paint color to the ceiling starting at the outside edge of the ceiling, where the wall meets the ceiling. Start just slightly left or right of a corner.

2 Immediately apply the existing ceiling paint color with a clean brush. Work the paint that is the ceiling color into the color of the halo paint using the French brush technique.

3 Blend the two colors together using the brush of the haloed color. Fade the haloed color out into the existing ceiling paint color.

Blend and soften the two colors while all paint is wet.

Continue around the room until you are done.

Note: If you work fast enough you will not have to use any water to loosen the paints up. However, if you find that the paints are drying way too quickly, first try to loosen the paints up by adding a third amount of water. If this does not help and the paints are merely being sucked into the surface, you probably are trying to paint over "ceiling paint." You will have to stop and repaint the ceiling in a high-quality latex or acrylic paint before continuing.

2 Metallic Paint

METALLIC PAINT can add drama and a touch of reflectivity to a ceiling. The nature of any metallic coating is to reflect light slightly; this is good news and this is bad news. What usually happens is that roller or brush marks are revealed in an undesirable way. This demonstration relies on the French brush method of application to create interest and beauty on a metallic surface by allowing you more control of the paint's movement during application.

Because you will be hand-brushing a ceiling area, another way to make your job easier is to first basecoat the ceiling in a flat latex paint that is very close in color to the metallic you have selected. The basecoat is applied in the conventional manner of cutting in the corners with a brush and rolling out the rest. This will save you from having to apply multiple coats of the metallic paint to achieve an opaque metallic finish coat.

Coverage of the basecoat should be pretty good but does not need to be perfect.

You may use a flat-edge paintbrush scaled to the size of your working area.

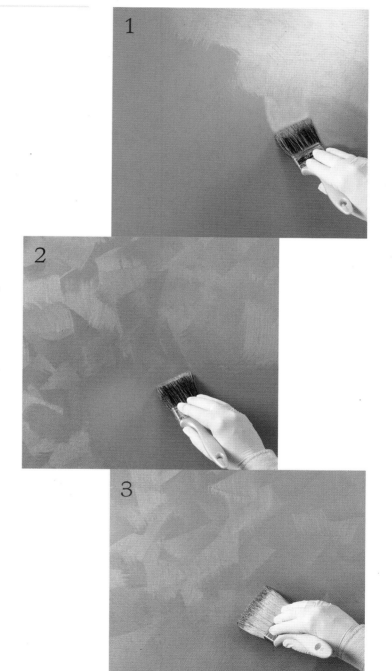

1 Notice how close the basecoat color is to the copper metallic.

Start to apply the copper metallic paint using the French brush technique.

2 Continue across your surface. It is always best to apply the metallic paint rather heavily and simply brush out without going over too much of what you have already painted on. Keep a wet edge.

3 Mix a few drops of equal amounts of Burnt Umber and Raw Umber UTC (see page 16) into satin oil varnish.

Apply in the same French brush manner a coat of tinted satin sheen oil varnish.

This varnish coat will help tone down the copper paint and will help even out some of the uneven sheen from your first application.

Remember, if you like your work without the tinted varnish applied, it is perfectly acceptable to not apply the tinted varnish.

Water-based varnishes will tend to crawl when applied over a metallic paint. That is why oil varnish is used.

3 Aluminum Roll Gilding

IF YOU do not want to apply many single sheets of aluminum leaf over your head to a ceiling in the traditional manner, there is an easier way: aluminum leaf comes on a roll! It is made just for this type of large, continuous surface application.

An aluminum-leafed ceiling is a spectacular finish.

It's wonderful for intimate rooms or even a large dining room where the lights from the chandelier can dance across this marvelous finish.

As with any gilding process, the final look is only as good as your prep, so make sure that your ceiling surface is smooth and free of any blemishes and cracks. The leaf will hide nothing.

Basecoat the ceiling to be leafed in a pale warm gray, eggshell-sheen latex paint applied with a foam roller to keep roller stipple to a minimum. The eggshell sheen will ensure proper sealing of the surface.

MATERIALS AND TOOLS

- water-based gold-leaf size
- flat latex paintbrush, 4" (10.2 cm)
- roller handles, 7" (17.8 cm)
- aluminum leaf on a roll
- spreading knife, 6" (15.25 cm)
- wallpaper blade
- lamb's wool pad
- denatured alcohol
- lint-free rag
- satin acrylic varnish

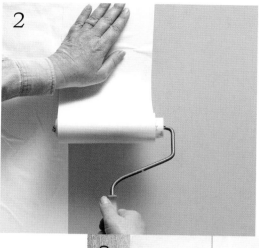

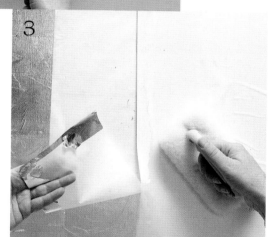

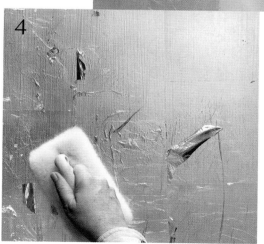

1 With a latex brush apply the size to an area of ceiling that you can comfortably gild in one day. Do not leave any skips.

Follow the instructions on the size bottle to know how long to wait before applying the leaf.

2 Start along the edge where the ceiling meets the wall to keep the roll of leaf straight.

With a 6" (15.25 cm) spreading knife, tuck the narrow side of the roll into the edge. Allow ½" (1.3 cm) excess to fall onto wall.

With mild tension, pull the roll of leaf at a 45° angle to the opposite side of the ceiling using your free hand to lightly press leaf to ceiling as you go.

When you are at the opposite wall, cut the leaf with a sharp wallpaper knife into the corner.

Overlap the previous row by ¼" (6 mm) and repeat until ceiling is covered.

3 With a lamb's wool pad, softly brush over the paper and the leaf. This will adhere the leaf, and the paper will fall off at this time.

4 Continue softly cleaning until all excess leaf is removed.

5 With a rag dampened with denatured alcohol, gently wipe the entire gilded surface down. This removes the wax on the surface of the leaf and allows your topcoat to be applied. Topcoat cannot be applied over the wax film.

6 With a good latex brush, apply a coat of satin acrylic varnish.

4 Venetian Plaster

THE BEAUTY OF Venetian Plaster is the rich, smooth, polished surface that results from the application and the burnishing. Multiple thin layers of the material applied with a special blade achieve the finish.

There are many good Venetian Plaster products on the market, just ask at your favorite paint store. The paint store should also sell the special blades with which to apply the material.

The demonstration shown here is the simple, basic technique with the added twist of using a second color to create a geometric pattern.

Picture this gleaming finish on a powder room ceiling.

For your basecoat color it is a good idea to generally apply a color close to the color of your plaster.

The ceiling surface should be smooth and without any imperfections as this plaster product will not cover imperfections due to the thinness of the application.

Follow the instructions found on the product that you buy, but know that basically you will be applying multiple thin coats of plaster and burnishing with a blade to create the polished look.

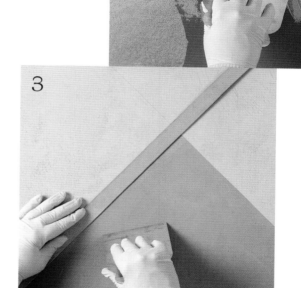

1 Apply the first coat of Venetian Plaster to the entire surface.

Using the special spreading blade, apply the material thinly and in short arched strokes that crisscross one another. Do not leave ridges; do not have all the blade strokes going the same direction.

Work quickly and do not go back over what you have already laid down.

2 Allow the first application to dry. Lightly run the blade over the surface to remove any burrs and apply a second application just as you did in step 1.

3 Allow the second coat to dry. With a chalk line make 2 diagonals from each corner of the ceiling.

You cannot tape Venetian Plaster, so hold a metal straightedge as your guide flat to the ceiling. Apply the darker material in the same manner you did the previous two applications.

You will have to keep moving the straightedge to create the line.

4 After the darker material has dried, apply a final coat of the light-colored Venetian Plaster to the entire surface.

The darker color will become softly buried under the lighter plaster.

5 Allow to fully dry. Polish the plaster with the blade held flat against the surface or sand with 800-grit wet/dry sandpaper to produce a beautiful polished stone look.

Tip: Practice your application on a sample board first. The plaster should go on thinly and smoothly in many layers to achieve the beauty of this product.

5 | Easy Sky

NOTHING SAYS "sky" like blue and white. If you are unsure of your cloud-making abilities, relax; you can achieve a believable sky-like painted ceiling in very quick fashion by simply using the French brush technique, outlined on page 16, by painting blue and white together.

Really, it is this easy. Remember that there are many types of natural skies and cloud formations so yours will indeed look like one found somewhere in nature.

When applying the colors always bring the white off the ceiling by having it appear to continue beyond the surface you are painting. This will give a more believable look of motion and expanse.

Due to the nature of the French brush technique you can generally paint over any well-painted ceiling as long as the color is not too far from white or blue. If you want to basecoat first, a coat of the light blue paint you will use can be applied. One coat should be sufficient, as you will be painting the surface again.

MATERIALS AND TOOLS

- flat latex paint, blue
- flat latex paint, white
- flat latex paintbrush, 3" (7.6 cm)

1 Liberally apply blue paint. Work within an area of your comfortable reach because you will want this blue paint to remain wet. You do not have to cover 100% of the surface but cover at least 70 to 80% of the surface.

2 Using the same paintbrush that you used to apply the blue paint, liberally apply the white paint, starting in the voids of the blue paint and brush into the wet blue paint. You may apply more blue too. Keep all paint wet.

3 While the blue and white colors are still wet, blend and soften the two paint colors together with the same paintbrush you have used to apply the blue and white.

Continue over the entire surface until complete. When you are done you will have a predominantly blue ceiling with softly folded-in areas of white that will suggest clouds.

6 Formal Sky

REALLY, it can be this easy! Just like the natural sky above us, there are all different kinds of clouds and skies. A windy day, a big billowy summer afternoon, even a dark and foreboding stormy sky.

This demonstration is for a windy day.

If you can do the Easy Sky on page 30, then you can do this technique because it is simply taking the Easy Sky a couple of steps further.

The only specific advice to remember is to take your clouds off the edges of the ceiling so they will look like they are passing through.

You may wish to clump a large cloud bank just slightly off-center or create a circular cloud pattern around your room.

You may want to add a few clouds cutting across the room at a slight angle in just one corner. The choice is yours.

Relax and picture yourself outside, or if it is a cloudy day, look outside for your inspiration!

1 French brush the blue and white together quickly.

2 Using the same paintbrush that you used to apply the blue and white paint, keep brushing the wet blue and white paint together to soften down any harsh brushstrokes, creating a softly mottled blue and white appearance.

3 When your blue and white paint has dried, look at the ceiling and see if you can start to see clouds. Focus on the light areas.

   With the paintbrush, pounce in cloud formations.

   Work within an area of your reach.

4 You may loosen the paint up a bit by dipping the brush into water.

   Go back into your cloud formations and soften the brushwork down.

   Remember, clouds generally have a bottom, so apply some of the blue paint to the bottom side and watch a cloud take shape.

   Create voluminous clouds or soft wispy ones; anything goes.

   Give your cloud very white highlights to suggest the sun.

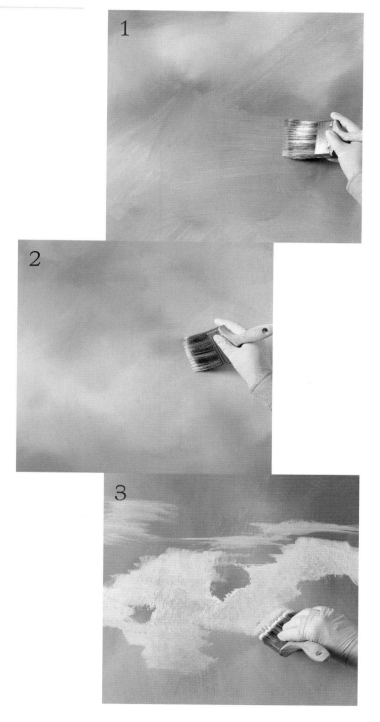

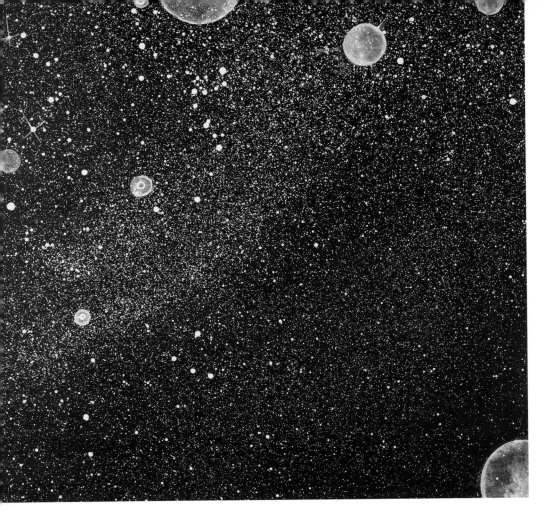

7 Celestial Sky

THE MYSTERY of a night sky painted right onto your ceiling can be a wonderful technique for children's rooms, libraries, powder rooms, or entry hall—just about anywhere you would want to see the stars.

For inspiration, look up "planetary and night sky images" on the Internet and you will soon discover that the sky is indeed the limit.

This can be a messy finish to apply so be sure to mask your room off with plastic and wear safety glasses and old paint clothes. Have fun creating the stars above and, oh, don't forget to wear a baseball cap!

- roller, 9" (23 cm)
- flat latex paint, deep midnight blue
- straight latex paintbrush, 4" (10.2 cm)
- spray bottle with adjustable nozzle

- flat latex paint, white
- paint pail
- flat latex paintbrush, 1" (2.5 cm)
- flat latex paintbrush, ¼" (6 mm)
- soft lint-free rag

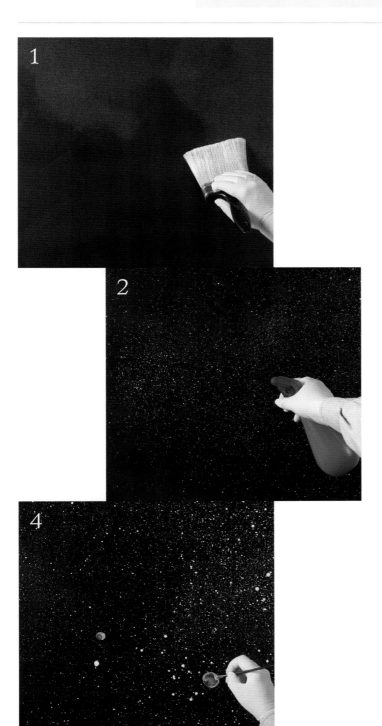

You will have to do 2 coats of the midnight blue in preparation for the stars. The first coat may be rolled on, but the second coat you will brush on.

1 After you have rolled out the first coat of blue paint and that coat has dried, apply the second coat with a brush.

Using a 4" (10.2 cm) flat latex brush, apply the second coat of blue paint using the French brush technique (page 16). The blue basecoat will be almost opaque, but not quite.

2 Mix a mixture of 60% flat white latex paint and 40% water in a paint pail and pour into a spray bottle.

Begin to apply the star matter. Set your spray bottle on the mist or spray setting, stand directly under the ceiling and softly squeeze the trigger until you get the feel of how the paint comes out.

You want a soft misting of star matter over entire surface.

3 Move a little closer to the surface, set your spray bottle to the stream setting, and gently squeeze the trigger to get a larger dot of paint.

You do not want a full stream of paint to come out; rather by squeezing gently you will get just a few larger dots of paint.

Coverage should be about 20 to 30% of entire surface area.

4 Use a ¼" (6 mm) paintbrush dipped into white paint and paint in a small planet.

Immediately press a lint-free rag into the center of the white paint to remove some of the paint, which will create the translucent quality.

Repeat with a 1" (2.5 cm) flat latex brush for larger planets.

8 | Leopard

YOU CAN PAINT LEOPARD, oh yes you can … and what fun you can have with it!

It is easy! It's basically blobs of paint going in a certain direction. We will call this direction: the growth direction, how the fur grows.

Imagine this technique on just about any ceiling. Whimsical and fanciful for a porch, kitchen, child's room, or even the master bedroom.

Read the description to #23, Floor Cloth, and make up a few of these to scatter throughout your home.

Do as many or as few "rosettes" as you wish. Make many smaller ones or fewer great big ones for a fantasy of leopard.

This technique is to have fun with, so pull out the paints, roll up your sleeves, and make you smile.

MATERIALS AND TOOLS

- latex flat paint, light beige/crème
- flat latex paintbrush, 3" (7.6 cm)
- flat latex paint, medium tawny beige
- flat paint, darker tawny beige
- angle-edged artist acrylic paintbrush, ¼" (6 mm)
- flat latex paint, black

1 Create the "undercoat." Down the middle, apply the light beige paint in a slight radial pattern.

   While the light beige paint is still wet, apply the medium tawny beige paint alongside and blend, keeping the slight radial pattern.

   Let the undercoat dry.

2 Apply the center of the rosettes by merely tapping the side of a ¼" (6 mm) brush that has been loaded with the dark tawny beige against the surface.

   Following the radial pattern, place more and smaller rosettes closer to the narrow portion of the undercoat and open fewer larger ones out toward the end.

   Mix in a few larger centers along the way.

   Allow the paint to dry completely.

3 With the ¼" (6 mm) paintbrush apply black paint around the dark tawny centers.

   Sort of "blob" the paint around the center portion.

   Leave one end open. Continue until you have your masterpiece.

Note: Practice a bit on paper to get the feel of your brush applying the black. It will come to you quickly.

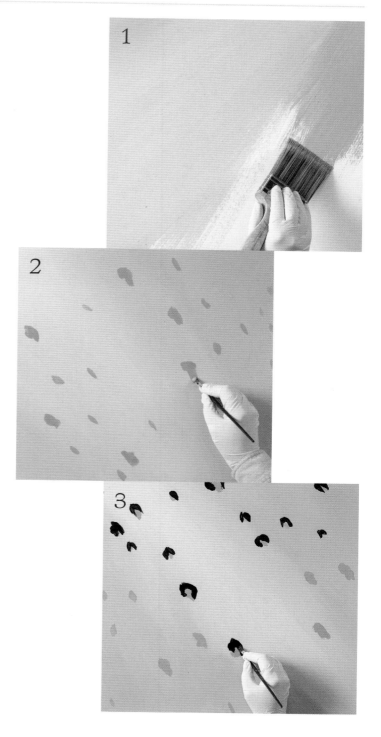

9 | Stamped Stars

LET CERTAIN MATERIALS and tools make your life easier! There are many great stamps on the market today, go out and find yourself a good star one.

A random placement has been selected for this demonstration, but you may follow a pattern if you wish. Select any basecoat color you want, but a deeper color seems to work best for this technique.

Always use solvent-based ink-pads so that your beautiful work is permanent. You may apply as many or as few stars as you would like, but I would caution against a 50/50 distribution. Imbalance and an asymmetrical distribution make for a more interesting total effect.

What makes this mere stamping of stars onto a ceiling more elegant is the addition of a shadow. The shadow will add depth and interest to the gold star on top of it. Usually a consistent light source is applied to the placement of a shadow, but in this application you do not have to concern yourself with this directional shading; just go forth and stamp away and enjoy yourself.

MATERIALS AND TOOLS

- star stamp
- solvent-based inkpad, black
- solvent-based inkpad, gold metallic

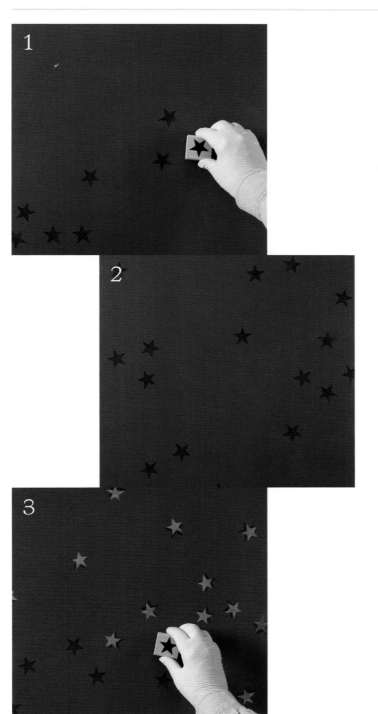

1 Start wherever you feel comfortable and apply all of the black star shadows first.
   The stamp should be solid and opaque.

2 Continue until you have a nice placement and are happy with it.

3 Allow the black stars to dry at least 4 hours. When the black stars are dry apply the gold stars.
   Make sure the stamp is replicating the black star's orientation.
   Offset the position of the gold star stamp slightly and stamp.
   Continue until all the black shadow stars have their top gold star.

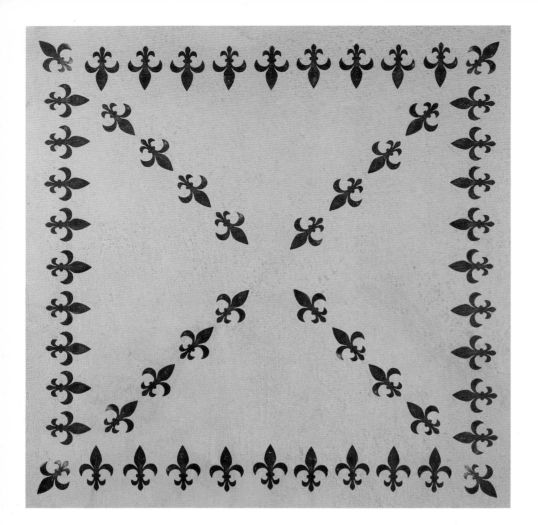

10 | Stamped Motifs

THE USE OF a stamp motif is a wonderful and easy way to see the beauty of a repetitive pattern.

Since stamps tend to be small, you may want to try this finish in a small powder room.

The inks for stamps come in a variety of beautiful colors and the only thing to keep in mind is to use a solvent-based inkpad. This will ensure a permanent pigment.

You will be using a chalk line here because you do not want a pencil mark. The chalk wipes off with a slightly water-dampened soft rag, although do not attempt to do so until all inks have been given an overnight dry.

The hardest thing for me when stamping is knowing where to put my next stamp so that everything comes out evenly spaced. I know that some stamps sometimes have little dots on them to indicate orientation, but I have never really come up with a good way to do even spacing, so I cannot tell you.

I just eyeball it and it seems to work pretty well for me. Remember: we are not machines.

The center was left blank in this demonstration, indicating where a light fixture would be.

MATERIALS AND TOOLS

- chalk line
- stamp with motif of your choice
- solvent-based inkpad, color of your choice
- water-based satin varnish
- UTC, Burnt Umber
- UTC, Raw Umber
- flat latex paintbrush, 4" (10.6 cm)
- cheesecloth, 90-weight

1 Find the center of the ceiling by snapping two diagonals chalk lines. Where they intersect is the middle.

Determine your border size and snap in chalk lines for those.

2 Begin in the center of the outside borderline and work to your left or right.

3 Allow the ink to dry overnight. To quietly soften the contrast and to protect your work, apply a coat of latex satin varnish tinted just a bit with UTC Burnt Umber and Raw Umber.

Brush on with the paintbrush and fold back with a pad of 90-weight cheesecloth. Remember to work quickly and keep a wet edge.

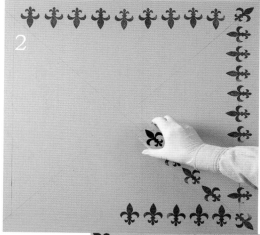

11 | Faux Drapery

THINGS THAT APPEAR difficult oftentimes are not.

This technique is wonderful for powder room ceilings, entries, or any other intimate ceiling. Yes, it can be done on a large ceiling, but practice first on a smaller ceiling.

The colors used in the demonstration are neutral, but you can always use a color such as red or deep blue if you choose. When selecting your color palette just remember that you will have three colors: the darkest, the medium, and the lightest.

Select a brush that is the appropriate size for the ceiling. In a powder room, a 2" (5.1 cm) or 3" (7.6 cm) angle-edged latex paintbrush would be an appropriate choice.

The drapery will come out of the center in a radial pattern and will be wider at the wall line and narrow at the center. Think of pie wedges. How wide you choose to make the drapery is up to you.

It is always easier to work the paints together when they are wet, so work in sections and then pull everything together at the end. Yes, you can go back into and over your work until you are satisfied.

- angle-edged latex paint-brush, size appropriate to surface area

- flat latex paint, almost black or warm black

- flat latex paint, medium warm black

- flat latex paint, white

- small pail of water

1 The darkest color radiates out from the center.

Brush in the undiluted warm black paint in a radial pattern.

The bulk of this color remains toward the center, but do pull some all the way out to the wall.

2 While the darkest color is still wet, and using the same paintbrush, paint the medium color into and alongside the dark color.

Do not completely cover the dark color.

Taper the medium color into the dark color.

Pull the medium color out to the wall edge more than you did the darkest color.

3 The white is applied with the same paint brush into the wet medium color and up into the darkest color.

Taper the paint into the center.

The application of the white into the other two darker colors will blend all three colors together.

Do not over-blend, as you do want to see some highlights from the white and some very deep lowlights from the darker colors.

Note: If you are having a difficult time keeping all the paints wet, you may set in the darkest so you have your pattern and go back and work in sections following the above steps.

The pail of water is used to "loosen" any of the paints by dipping your brush into the water just a bit and picking up your paint.

You do not need to nor should you clean the brush between colors.

12 Large Graphic

WHAT DOESN'T look like much can become much. A large graphic applied to a large, otherwise blank ceiling can add interest and "architecture" to a room. The demonstration outlined on these pages is rendered in a soft color palette suggesting "shadows." This design features a very close color palette, which in effect slowly pulls the viewer's eye upward.

If you would like to use a very bold color palette, feel free to do so. Consider mimicking the pattern onto your floor in one of the other techniques outlined in this book.

Picture, if you will, this ceiling graphic applied and then you stencil large floor designs onto your floor using the same design, or copy the ceiling's design to relate the two surfaces of floor and ceiling together.

This can create a very understated impact of the pattern.

The key to this technique is finding the center of the ceiling and building the design out from that point, as walls are generally never perfectly straight and you want the center to indeed be the center of the ceiling.

MATERIALS AND TOOLS

- chalk line
- measuring tape
- painter's tape and paper
- flat latex paint, very pale blue
- flat latex paint, very pale green
- paint roller appropriate to size of pattern

1 To find the center of your ceiling, snap a chalk line diagonally from corner to corner.

Using the center point, define the center square or rectangle if your room is rectangular. Simply measure out from the center point the same distance on all 4 diagonals and connect the dots with the chalk line.

2 Set in the very pale blue corners by again measuring from the diagonals an equal distance on all 4 diagonals and make the squares the size you wish. Generally the design looks better if you leave a border of base color between the edge of the square and the wall.

3 Mask off the center square and apply the very pale green to the center.

Wait for all paint to dry and wash off or brush off the remaining chalk lines.

Tip: When taping off the chalk lines, run the tape just along the outside of the chalk line, leaving the chalk line on the inside of the tape so that when you paint, the chalk line is erased by the paint.

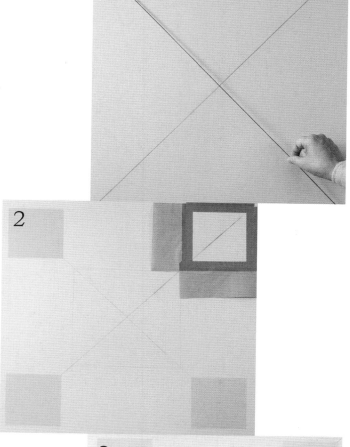

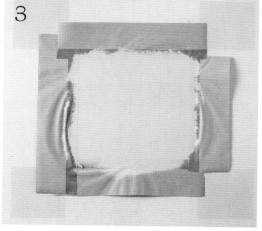

13 | Applied Leaf Motifs

UNLESS YOU ARE a wonderful pictorial artist and can merely freehand paint these leaves in, you might not think that you can get a pictorial to look as nice as this. But you can. You can use stamps, handmade stencils, and a little bit of painting in to do the job easily and beautifully.

This demonstration will provide you with a quick and easy way to paint a leaf canopy peeking out of the corners onto the ceiling.

To make this job effortless, use stamps and stencils to quickly determine where you want your leaves to go. A composition will always look better if it looks random. Think in terms of asymmetrical placement. You might want to bunch up more leaves in only one corner of the room and allow the other corners to have fewer leaves painted in. You do not have to cover each of the four edges of your ceiling; instead let the motifs meander and roam and suddenly appear.

Remember to have on hand some of the basecoat paint just in case you might want to "erase" an errant leaf.

Some brushwork will be involved and will be demonstrated to show you quickly how to use your brush to paint in the stamped and stenciled leaves.

- stamp of leaves
- solvent-based inkpad, dark green
- stencil material

- X-Acto knife
- stencil brush
- angle-edged artist acrylic paintbrush, ¼" (6 mm)

- flat latex paint, dark green
- flat latex paint, black
- flat latex paint, white

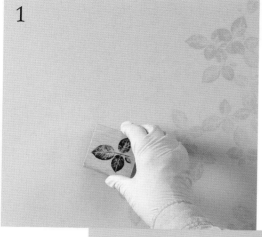

1

1 Use the leaf stamp to start the design of your foliage.

Stamp as many or as few as you wish.

2 Add the stenciled leaves. Cut out 3 leaves from a good blank piece of stencil material: a large one, medium one, and small one.

Apply the leaf stencils randomly and over the stamped leaves.

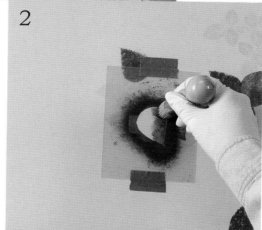

2

3 On a piece of paper, practice making the small strokes that you will use to paint in your leaves. This stroke will work for the larger leaves too; you will just have to paint in more.

Color mix your black, green, and white paint with your paintbrush as you go to vary the tones of green.

Do this by merely picking up some black and green for the darkest, just green for the mid-tone, and green with some white for the lightest leaves.

4 When you are comfortable, proceed to the ceiling.

Remember to vary the colors of green leaves. Some leaves will be dark while others will be pale. This will create depth and interest.

3

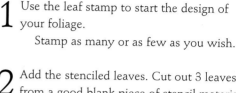

14 Elaborate Stencil

THE LOOK of a hand-painted ceiling corner, border, or center embellishment can be achieved by using a stencil as a guide.

Remember that a stencil is broken up only to form bridges that hold the stencil together. You will simply be mending some of those bridges to create a more hand-painted look. Positive space is simply the space that is filled in.

You will notice in this demonstration that the stencil is a light and "feathery" one. If this were to be applied just as is to a ceiling, the beautiful design might become lost. Remember that artwork applied to a ceiling tends to disappear due to the overhead position of the ceiling. Therefore, this type of stencil would lend itself to a bit of "beefing up" so the pattern becomes more distinguishable.

By filling in certain areas within the stencil, this positive (filled in) space becomes an important element of the design and composition. Look for those that have an interesting shape.

Even the most intricate or minimal stencil can benefit from this technique.

The following demonstration is for use of the stencil as a border along the outside edge of the ceiling.

MATERIALS AND TOOLS

- pencil
- large wall or ceiling stencil
- spray can of temporary fixative
- measuring tape

- flat latex paint
- foam roller brush and roller handle, 4" (10.2 cm)
- small paint tray

- stencil brush
- artist angle-edged acrylic paintbrush, ½" (1.3 cm)
- small round artist detail paintbrush

1 Determine the middle of your border. Do this by finding the middle of the ceiling as it runs along the wall.

2 Draw a perpendicular line the depth of the stencil to the wall line in pencil.

3 Spray the back of the stencil with a low-tack temporary adhesive. This will help keep the stencil in place on the ceiling. You will have to periodically reapply.

4 Line up the center of the stencil along the perpendicular line you drew designating the center and begin to paint. The use of a small foam roller to apply the paint over the stencil will make your job easier.

Load the roller, off-roll a couple of times, and gently roll over the stencil with the loaded roller.

5 Continue applying the stencil along the perimeter of your ceiling until you have finished. Make sure to mark the registration marks that are found on most high-quality stencils.

When you have completed the border, look at the design and if you like it, you are done! If you would like to liven it up a bit, begin to paint in logical sections. Do the same sections around the entire border.

Notice how filling in and connecting lines changes the attitude of the stencil.

Note: I oftentimes buy two stencils so that, if need be, I can cut one for the corners.

Note: If you do not want to spend all this time on a ladder, simply make your own border as done in Cambric Cloth (page 58).

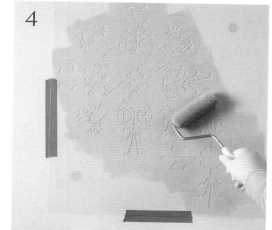

15 | Decorative Molding

ANY CEILING likes a little pick-me-up. Simply adding a decorative piece of molding to a ceiling and exercising some color changes can take a simple plain ceiling to a sophisticated statement.

This technique is beautiful on large living room and/or dining room ceilings.

It softens a bedroom ceiling and gives you something to look at while you are lying in bed.

You might want someone who is really good at measuring and sawing wood to do the cutting. A chop saw is handy for the cutting part. Simple miter cuts are what you need to make and the seams can be filled with caulk if they do not fit perfectly. But once the molding is up and the nails holes filled, it is time to dress the ceiling up.

Prime the wood molding before you apply it to the ceiling. This will make painting it easier.

This technique is based on a color formula to get different shades of the same color, which will give depth and interest to the ceiling area and still maintain an overall color palette.

- decorative ceiling molding, cut and installed

- appropriate amount of the darkest color flat latex paint

- equal amount of flat white paint

- paint pail

- angle-edged latex paintbrush, 2" (5.1 cm)

- angle-edged latex paintbrush, 2½" (6.4 cm)

- paint rollers for larger areas

1 Take the darkest paint and pour some into a separate pail and add to that amount an equal part of the white paint. This will be your molding color and the lightest color.

Paint the molding first, as it is detailed, and do not worry if you get some paint on the ceiling, as you will be painting that, too.

2 Apply the darkest color to the outside perimeter of the ceiling. Practice cutting in so you have no need for tape.

3 Pour some of the darkest color into a pail and to that add one-quarter of the amount of white paint. This will be the center of the ceiling color.

Apply to center of ceiling.

You can see that you will use mostly the dark color, so purchase accordingly and always use the same white paint to mix your colors with, as there are many different whites in a paint line.

You could just buy the three colors that are next to one another on a color deck, but doing the color mixing this way creates a softer, less discernible sophisticated color shift on your ceiling.

16 Faux Tin Ceiling

THERE ARE A FEW heavily embossed wall coverings on the market today that have patterns resembling tin ceilings. These wall coverings are usually made from a paper pulp material and need to be painted. Indeed they need to be painted with a flat latex paint.

The embossed material is hung like most wall coverings. Always follow manufacturer's instructions for proper installation and priming.

These heavily embossed textures will not hide a horrible ceiling surface, but will cover up minor imperfections and truly give a very elegant and special look to a ceiling.

Try it in a small powder room or a smaller entry for that special touch of importance to an otherwise ignored ceiling surface. Or, feel free to apply to larger areas. The choice is yours!

MATERIALS AND TOOLS

- deeply embossed wall covering
- flat latex paint for basecoat, pale gray
- flat latex paintbrush, 4" (10.2 cm)
- metallic latex paint, silver or aluminum-colored
- satin oil-based varnish
- UTC, Burnt Umber
- UTC, Raw Umber
- UTC, Raw Sienna
- flat oil paintbrush, 4" (10.2 cm)
- small flat block
- mineral spirits
- cheesecloth, 90-weight
- respirator(s) for vapors and fumes

1 Basecoat the material according to manufacturer's instructions in a pale gray color.

2 Select one of the many high-quality silver or aluminum-colored latex metallic paints available on today's market.

Brush on liberally to get into all the low points. Metallic paint should be opaque and solid covering.

3 Tint satin oil varnish with mostly Burnt Umber, half of that amount with Raw Umber, and half of that amount with Raw Sienna UTCs (page 16). Add about a quarter amount of mineral spirits to loosen the varnish up. Add tint slowly. The color should be transparent.

4 You cannot remove the varnish glaze while it is wet. Let the varnish dry just until it loses its high sheen. When it has, usually within half an hour, you are ready to remove the glaze from the high points of the embossed pattern.

To do so, wrap a block that you can comfortably hold in your hand in a few layers of 90-weight cheesecloth. You want the surface that you will use to remove the glaze to be firm and flat so that it only removes the glaze from the high points.

Carefully rub the cheesecloth-wrapped block over the surface, removing glaze from high points, adjusting the pressure as necessary to remove the glaze. When your cloth gets too dirty, simply re-wrap to a cleaner side.

WEAR A RESPIRATOR! when you work with the oil-based varnish because you will be very close to the ceiling where the fumes like to collect.

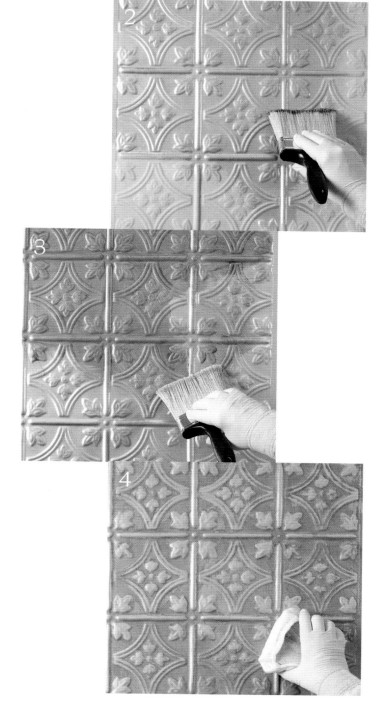

17 Antiqued Embossed Material

THE MAIN difference between this technique and the Faux Tin Ceiling (page 52) is that you will be using a flat latex paint instead of a metallic latex paint. Think in terms of color with this technique. By adding color and texture to your ceiling, you can add interest and even depth to an otherwise overlooked ceiling surface.

Always follow the manufacturer's installation instructions.

Picture this technique elegantly enhancing a small yet special powder room or even an open and otherwise blank kitchen ceiling.

Another difference with this technique as opposed to the tin ceiling technique is that in step 2 you will be "folding" the satin oil-based varnish glaze back into the surface by texturing with a cheesecloth rag.

You will be using UTCs to tint the varnish glaze, so remember that UTCs go a long way, as does the varnish when you brush it out.

For 1 quart (1 liter) of the tinted varnish, start with a small squirt of the green UTC and about a third of that of Raw Umber UTC. Always add colorant slowly so you do not over-tint.

MATERIALS AND TOOLS

- deeply embossed wall covering
- flat latex paint for basecoat
- flat latex paintbrush, 4" (10.2 cm)
- satin oil-based varnish
- UTC, Permanent Green
- UTC, Raw Umber
- flat oil paintbrush, 4" (10.2 cm)
- cheesecloth, 90-weight
- small flat block
- mineral spirits
- respirator(s) for vapors and fumes

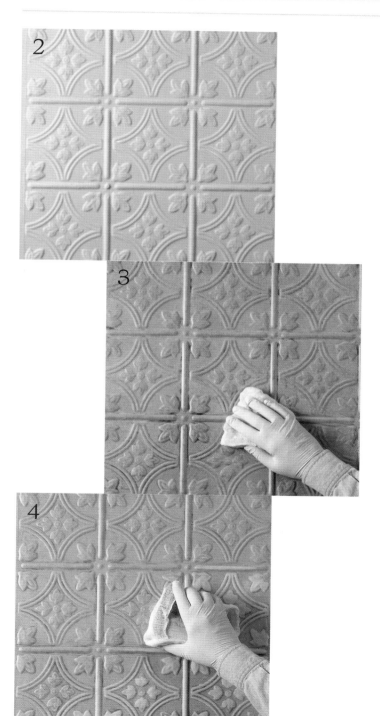

1 Apply the flat latex basecoat paint with the latex paintbrush. Generally lighter colors work best for basecoat, darker colors for glazing medium.

2 Mix your satin varnish glaze by adding a small amount of UTC Permanent Green tint to oil-based satin oil varnish and "dull" the green down a bit by adding a smaller amount of UTC Raw Umber. Add a shy quarter amount of mineral spirits to the varnish.

Apply tinted varnish to a workable area of the ceiling. Remember to keep a wet edge.

3 To remove brushstrokes and fold the varnish into the surface, pounce softly with a pad of 90-weight cheesecloth. Continue to brush on tinted varnish and pounce to soften until the whole area is covered.

This will help even out the varnish and help it set up.

4 Once the varnish has lost its high-gloss sheen and has dulled out, you may start to remove the varnish glaze from the high points. Carefully rub the cheesecloth-wrapped block over the surface, removing glaze from high points and adjusting the pressure as necessary to remove the glaze. When your cloth gets too dirty, simply re-wrap to a cleaner side.

Note: Wear a respirator that is approved for vapors and fumes.

18 | Ceiling Medallion

THINK OF THESE as jewelry for your ceiling. Adding a ceiling medallion around a light fixture can be the perfect added accessory that finishes the "outfit." Once painted, these Styrofoam medallions certainly can be impressive. A visitor would be hard pressed to distinguish it from an old plaster medallion.

The good news is, you can sit and watch television while you make this wonderful little treasure. Patience and a fairly steady hand, along with a couple of good brushes, is all it takes.

The color palette chosen for this demonstration is a subtle one, but yours could be as festive as colorful Italian pottery if you so desire. In the example shown here there is also a play of sheens happening. The basecoat is flat, the acanthus leaves (the big beige leaves) are eggshell, and the metallic rope is semigloss. When the medallion is hung with a light in the center, this interplay of sheens will be lovely.

Putting the medallion on a lazy Susan helps. You will get familiar with painting in with one stroke, using the shape of the brush.

MATERIALS AND TOOLS

- flat latex paint, green

- oval sash paintbrush, 2" (5.1 cm)

- eggshell latex paint, beige

- flat latex paint, deep green

- metallic latex paint, champagne

- flat latex paint, rust

- angle-edged high-quality acrylic artist paintbrush, ¼" (6 mm)

1 Apply the green basecoat to the entire piece. Use the oval sash paintbrush and pounce the flat green latex paint on, making sure to get all crevices. The coat does not have to be opaque and solid covering; if you see a bit of the white factory basecoat coming through, that is desirable.

Allow to dry.

2 Apply the eggshell sheen latex beige paint to the acanthus leaves. Coat should be solid covering.

3 Apply the latex metallic champagne color to the rope section. Coat should be solid.

4 Paint in the deep green to the grape leaves. Coat should be solid.

5 Paint the rust onto the grapes.

19 Cambric Cloth

IT REALLY CAN be this simple…

Cambric cloth is the material most window shades are made out of. This cloth makes a wonderful material to cut and apply to a ceiling, just as you would any wallpaper. The material may be first painted, gilded, stenciled, or anything else you may think of. The nice thing about this technique is that you can do the majority of your artwork down on a worktable, because you will install the final product, as you would wallpaper.

Ask at your local paint store which of the wallpaper adhesives would be the best to use.

Another wonderful attribute is that the material is extremely easy to remove when you want to change.

The technique outlined here is a free-form approach using cutouts of squares and rectangles. You may want to sketch out a basic design on paper first, but this technique is much more fun if you just "go for it." In other words: do not think too much and you will find that a beautiful design begins to take shape.

Consistent inconsistency along with the contemporary use of shape and color is what this technique is all about.

MATERIALS AND TOOLS

- cambric cloth
- flat latex paint, colors of your choice
- flat latex paintbrush, 4" (10.2 cm)
- wallpaper knife
- straightedge
- triangle
- wallpaper paste
- sponge
- paint pail

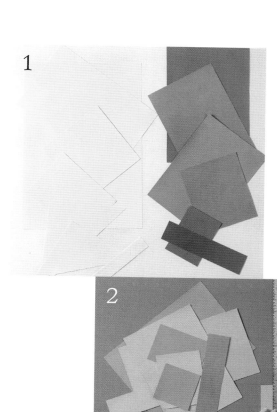

1 The cambric cloth will come on a roll most likely 36" (91.4 cm) wide by however long you request, so the first thing you want to do is cut the material down into manageable sizes. Once you have done that, simply paint your different colors on with a paintbrush.

2 When the pieces are dry, you may begin to cut up the material into sizes and shapes you like. Sometimes it helps to set your corners in first as a mild form of direction. If you want pieces of the same size but different colors, simply put one piece over the other and double-cut.

3 Use tape to test-fit the pieces to the ceiling to map out your design if you wish. Paste the pieces into their final position. Use a wallpaper knife to flatten the pieces to the ceiling.

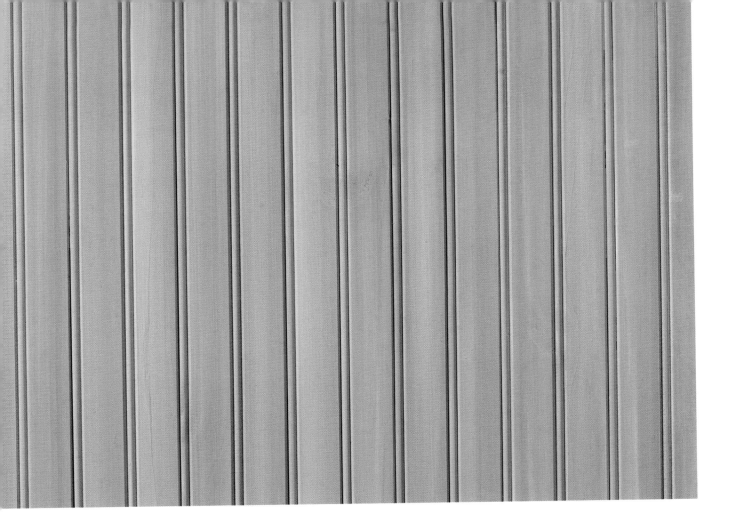

20 | Weathered Beadboard

THIS FINISH is perfect for the boat-house—if you are lucky enough to have one! If not, this is a lovely finish for a porch ceiling or a dado in your kitchen.

This technique demonstrates blending deep colors together with lighter colors to create depth and interest in the final result.

If the beadboard surface is not painted, no need to prime first. If the beadboard surface is painted and you do not know with what, apply a latex bonding primer before applying your colors.

The influence of the deeper colors may not be all that apparent in the final photo, but rest assured that on a larger surface area you will see the influence. You can control the amount of that influence by how much and how heavily you apply the lighter colors.

The deeper underneath colors will produce a subtle shading and depth to the final lighter colors.

1 Apply the green and red with a 3" (7.6 cm) brush and blend together a bit. Do not think too much. Leave the grooves the darkest.

Paint is used straight from the can, but occasionally dip your brush in some water to loosen everything up a bit if your paint is drying too quickly.

2 When the green and red paint are dry, use a 3" (7.6 cm) brush to apply the blue and white together.

The more often you dip your brush in the water, the looser the paints will be.

The looser the paints, the more transparent they are.

Use the water to vary the degree of transparency of the blue and white.

3 When all paints are dry, prepare a "whitewash" by mixing 1 part white paint to 2 parts water. With a 4" (10.2 cm) brush, apply the wash for a slightly "chalky" look.

21 Beadboard Stained & Antiqued

IF YOU ARE FACED with a large expanse of a beadboard installation, this is a quick and painless way to achieve a beautifully stained and antiqued look, which will bring a warm coloration and interest to the room.

Woodworker's stores and high-quality paint stores now carry interesting lines of water-soluble dyes that come in colors other than just the standard browns. Simply mix the dye solution with water to make your solution.

These dyes will work only over unfinished wood surfaces.

Due to the intensity of the colors, this demonstration shows you how to tone down the color and give a slight suggestion of age. Remember that color on the ceiling tends to appear darker so the richness of the tinted varnish will help to deepen and add richness to the bright vibrant color dye.

The products used in this demonstration are all water-based.

Be sure to follow manufacturer's instructions.

MATERIALS AND TOOLS

- water-soluble dye
- measuring cup
- flat latex paintbrush, 3″ (7.6 cm)
- water-based satin polyurethane
- UTC, Raw Umber
- UTC, Burnt Umber
- UTC, Raw Sienna

1 Mix the dye with water according to manufacturer's instructions. If you want a deeper color you may mix with less water.

It is always wise to have a sample piece of wood handy to test color.

Start at top if you are working on a slanted ceiling and be careful not to drip dye onto surfaces below you.

Brush in a back-and-forth manner to evenly distribute the material.

Work the length of the surface; do not skip around. Brush from end to end.

Simply brush on and feather into completed section as you continue.

2 Continue applying the dye. Let the grooves work for you. Cut into the grooves as you proceed, using the groove to guide your paintbrush.

3 Allow an overnight dry period to make sure everything is dry. Then apply a water-based satin polyurethane tinted with just a few drops of UTC Raw Umber, a little less of UTC Burnt Umber, and even less UTC Raw Sienna.

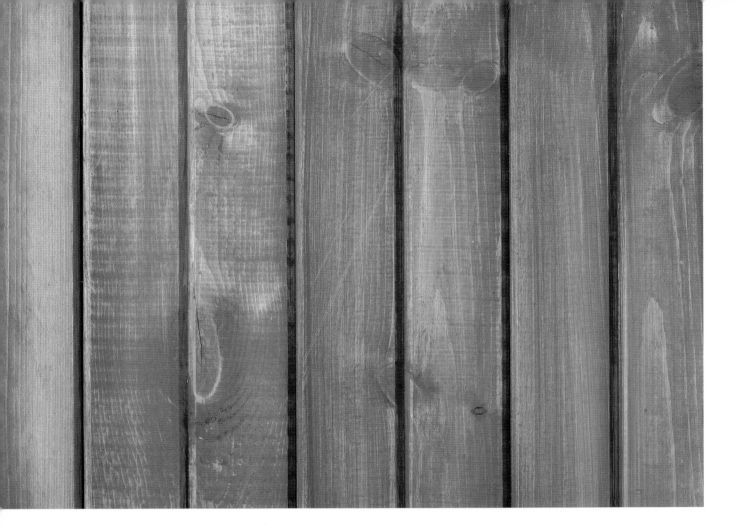

22 Stained Knotty Pine

KNOTTY PINE PLANKS are often used for and make a lovely ceiling material. Found in cabins and even urban homes, it makes for a good ceiling material where installing sheetrock would be difficult and time-consuming, as the planks fit together with a tongue-and-groove assemblage and the thickness hides a myriad of unfinished area difficulties.

Try installing in that third floor you have been meaning to finish off.

If the wood is slightly stained or just clear-coated, the look is fresh and clean. However, if it is the look of age you are after, this technique will make you happy.

Picture a final result that looks as if it has been there awhile. With the warm glow of time you can see this finish complementing a beautiful wood floor with a warm rug and an inviting fire in the fireplace beckoning you to bring your book and curl up.

MATERIALS AND TOOLS

- flat oil paint, Raw Sienna
- mineral spirits
- 2 flat oil paintbrushes, 3" (7.6 cm)
- gel stain, Dark Walnut
- lint-free rags

1 Thin the Raw Sienna oil paint with one-third mineral spirits. Apply the Raw Sienna-colored flat oil paint to the flat portion of the plank with the paintbrush. Be liberal with the amount of paint.

2 Along the still-wet Raw Sienna oil paint, tuck the Dark Walnut gel stain into the groves of the plank.

3 While everything is still wet, blend the paint and stain together, allowing the darker gel stain to hold in the crevices.
   Continue until all surface area is done.
   Apply a satin oil varnish topcoat if so desired for a beautiful gleam or just leave for a more rustic look.

Tip: You do not want the materials to dry out, so work along the whole length of a couple of planks. As you continue, the oil paint will blend into the finished area, but it is best to keep your work neat and end with the Dark Walnut wiped out of a crevice; then move on with the Raw Sienna-colored paint.

Note: Dispose of staining rags in airtight water-filled container so they do not spontaneously combust.

Fantastic
FLOORS

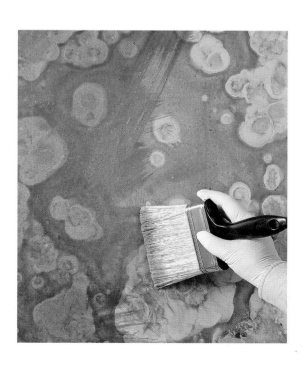

23 Floor Cloth

THIS DEMONSTRATION will show you how to make a floor cloth out of basic, everyday sheet vinyl.

Home improvement stores sell large and small pre-cut rolls of vinyl and what is on the face of this vinyl does not matter, as you will be using the back of it!

The historical way of making a floor cloth out of canvas can be believably emulated by simply using the backside of vinyl. No pasting edges down and "blocking" canvas.

Vinyl is easy to cut, has a crisp edge that will not fray, and is easy to find. You could even try hot-gluing some fringe to the underside edge if you want. Place a rug gripper pad under your floor cloth when you are done and it really will stay in place.

The stencil used in this demonstration is for a medallion motif. When selecting a floor stencil, look for the images that would lend themselves to a medallion design.

This floor cloth is perfect for outdoor or indoor use; just be sure to use the appropriate paints and topcoats.

MATERIALS AND TOOLS

- vinyl sheet
- utility knife
- metal straightedge
- latex bonding primer
- flat latex paint, black
- flat latex paint, green

- medium value flat latex paint, beige
- flat latex paintbrush, 4" (10.2 cm)
- floor stencil
- white chalk pencil

- foam roller brush, 4" (10.2 cm)
- roller handle, 4" (10.2 cm)
- small circle stencil
- flat stencil brush, ½" (1.3 cm)
- latex satin polyurethane

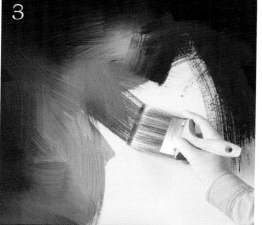

1 Cut your vinyl to the desired size with a very sharp utility knife and a metal straightedge.

2 Prime the backside of the vinyl sheet with a white latex-bonding primer.

3 Apply your background color using the French brush technique. Try to keep the center area of your "canvas" lighter and the edges darker. This application will give you a slightly mottled background that will make your overall result look a bit more mysterious.

4 Find the center of your "canvas" and draw a line with a white chalk pencil through it in each direction.

Your canvas will now have 4 sections.

5 Begin to apply the stencil by lining up the registration mark with the center point and line you have drawn.

Use the foam roller to apply the paint.

Load the roller and off-load a bit. You do not want a heavily loaded roller when you apply to the stencil.

Roll from the bottom up and out.

Be sure you have transferred the registration marks and continue until all 4 sections are painted in.

6 Once the medallion stencil is painted, it is nice to add a little something to the center and to the corners. A circle will be used to do so.

Use a small circle stencil and small stencil brush to apply.

With a water-dampened rag, remove any visible pencil lines.

7 Apply two coats of latex satin sheen polyurethane for floors.

24 Jute Monogram

WANT TO MAKE a statement on your rug? You can use stencils to say whatever you might want to express; this demonstration outlines a traditional monogram.

Fabric paint is used on the jute material. Fabric paint comes in heat-sensitive and nonheat-sensitive; use the nonheat sensitive. This simply means that you do not have to apply heat to set the paint. Explore your craft store for fabric paint and look for a fuller-bodied paint as opposed to a fabric paint that is very thin.

This technique may also be applied to cotton rugs or sisal and is a great way to have some fun and/or sophistication.

The only thing to keep in mind is that you really have only one chance to make your statement, so think before you speak. Take the time to make a mock-up first to check placement, measurements and spacing. This will save you any surprises on your rug.

- rug
- stencil alphabet the size you wish
- ruler
- triangle
- green tape (will stick to hard-to-stick surfaces)
- medium stiff stencil paintbrush, ¾" (1.9 cm)
- nonheat-sensitive full-bodied fabric paint, black

1 Make a mock-up of the monogram.

2 Measure where you want the bottom line of your letters to be. This line should not be dead center, rather make the bottom space an extra ¼" (6 mm) to ½" (1.3 cm) larger. Just as you would in matting a picture, do so here, as the slightly more space at the bottom will visually allow the monogram to appear more centered.

Also set a side line where your letter will begin. Use a triangle to make sure the bottom and side line create a 90° angle.

Use your mock-up to make sure everything will be where you want it to be.

3 Begin to apply the letters one letter at a time.

Line the edge of letter stencil along the edge of side line.

Line the bottom of letter stencil along edge of bottom line.

Use green tape to hold stencil in place.

Softly pounce the paint on with the stencil brush, starting in the center and off-loading a bit before moving to the edges.

Stencil in all the letters one at a time.

4 After you have all the letters applied, you may or may not like the look of a stenciled letter. If you do you are done, if not you may use the edge of a stencil to fill in.

Simply lay the stencil along a letter edge and stencil in gap to about half the letter's thickness.

Be careful not to extend paint too far into center at interior angles.

Hold the stencil edge along the opposite edge of letter and complete the filling in.

Fill in all gaps and you are now complete.

Allow paint to fully dry before use.

25 | Diamonds on the Floor

IT'S ALL ABOUT the tape! Let the tape work for you. This demonstration is done over a pre-fabricated floor and the wood showing will be part of the design.

If you have a tired old wood floor and want to freshen it up and change the look of the room, this technique will do just that.

It's good for porches, kitchens, anywhere really where you will be seeing the whole, or most of, the floor, because this technique is an all-over pattern. After you have spent all that time on your knees, you will want to see your lovely work.

The color in the demonstration is a light neutral color, suggesting informality, but as an alternative imagine this design done in warm black with small white squares for a more formal feel.

- ruler
- chalk line
- black marker or white pencil
- lacquer thinner (if using black marker)

- painter's tape, 2" (5.1 cm)
- latex bonding primer
- latex floor paint in color of your choice
- foam roller brush

- roller extension pole
- straight paintbrush appropriate for topcoat
- satin polyurethane for topcoat
- metal straightedge

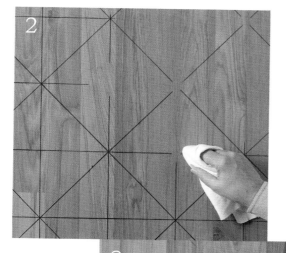

1 Find the center of your floor. Begin in the center and mark off the desired size of the diamond. Be sure you center the first diamond over the center.

Mark your measurement off all the way around the room and draw connecting lines from each one.

To form the diamond, draw in on the diagonal the measurement you want. Connect all the diagonals.

2 Erase the unnecessary lines. Lacquer thinner will remove permanent marker if that is what you used. Always do a test first to make sure whatever you used to make the lines can be easily removed from the exposed wood floor.

3 Tape off all the diamonds you want to paint. Mark them with a little bit of tape.

Your tape should be placed so that the line will be painted over.

Lay the tape down fairly smoothly and you will see your smaller diamond form.

Be sure to burnish down all tape edges securely, using an old credit card (saves your fingernails).

4 Apply your primer. The best way is to use a foam roller. Attach the roller handle to a roller extension pole or a broom handle so you can stand up and paint.

Allow to dry.

5 Apply your paint coat. Once the paint has dried, carefully remove the tape. If the paint is pulling the paint off the floor, put a straightedge down and first score the paint along the tape edge.

6 After all paint has dried, apply one or two coats of satin polyurethane.

26 Bubbles

WHY NOT HAVE bubbles on your floor? This amusing technique is as fun to do as the result. There is no pattern to follow; just let your eye lead you. Consideration of where furniture and rugs may go would be the only thing you might want to pay attention to.

It is easy to give a bit of volume to a circle by adding a highlight. Voilà, a flat circle becomes a dimensional "bubble."

When you are done applying all the bubbles, topcoat the entire floor. This will not only protect your artwork, but something else very interesting happens as well. When you look at the floor from a distance and at an angle you might not see much, but when you get above the bubbles and look down you certainly will. This is a nice effect and a fun discovery.

Or, you may just topcoat your bubbles to protect your artwork.

MATERIALS AND TOOLS

- latex bonding primer, tinted dark gray
- flat latex paint, white
- flat latex paint, black
- 3 circle stencils: I large, I medium, I small
- 2 medium stiff stencil brushes

1 Prime in your circles using the different size circles. Allow the primer to dry.

2 Apply a "crescent" of white paint over the primed circle.

3 While the black and white paints are still wet, blend the black into and softly over the white. Do not obliterate the white, but rather softly blend the two colors together to have a light spot.

Note: It is always easier to apply dark into light. Practice a bit first with the shading; you will get it. The use of a stencil will help you to not load your brush too much and this will make the blending easier.

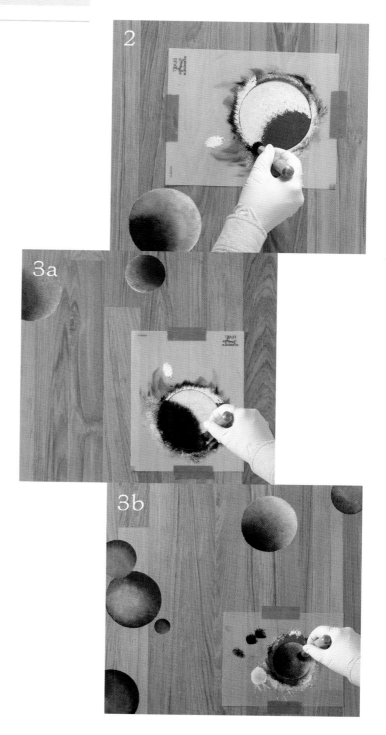

27 Distressed Painted Hardwood Floor

THE WARMTH AND BEAUTY of age is what this demonstration reveals. This finish may be applied over an old and worn hardwood floor or a new and shiny prefabricated floor, changing either of them into a beautiful old and worn look that says, "I have been here a long time."

This is a great fix for hardwood floors you do not want to refinish just yet, or to make a prefabricated floor far more interesting. This technique is a delightful way to alter the look of your floor to fit in better with your décor and bring a change of attitude to your room.

Before any paint is applied, the surface must be clean and free of any wax buildup and scuff-sanded.

Because this finish requires the use of paint stripper, work in a well-ventilated room and always use gloves and safety glasses. There are some very good water-based low-odor paint strippers on the market today; be sure to find one.

- flat latex paint, beige
- hair dryer (optional)
- flat latex paint, white
- flat latex paintbrush, 4" (10.2 cm)

- flat latex paintbrush, 3" (7.6 cm)
- paint stripper
- gloves
- lint-free rag

- low-sheen water-based floor polyurethane
- UTC, Raw Umber
- UTC, Burnt Umber
- lamb's wool applicator

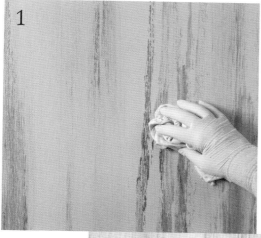

1 Selectively brush on some of the beige paint. Do not paint beige paint on 100% of the surface.

Work in an area you are comfortable with. When the beige paint has begun to dry out and is matte (paint can be forced dry with a hairdryer), use your smaller brush to selectively brush on some of the paint stripper.

Begin to wipe out the stripper, selectively removing some of the paint.

You want the stripper and paint to be able to be rubbed slightly off, leaving paint residue.

Continue to treat the entire surface in this manner.

2 Repeat step 1 only with the white paint. You want some of the beige color to show through and you want some of the white to remain.

3 Tint water-based polyurethane with a little Raw Umber and Burnt Umber.

After all paints have dried, apply a coat of the lowest sheen water-based polyurethane you can find for floors.

If the area to be topcoated is not large, use the 4" (10.2 cm) flat latex paintbrush; if the area is large, apply polyurethane with a lint-free lamb's wool applicator.

Note: Why not just put both colors selectively on and then use the paint stripper? The reason each coat is treated separately is because you want the floor to look like layers of different colors of paint have worn through and you do not want the stripper to be applied to paint that is too dry. You may certainly try to do it that way. But the outlined way will create a more subtle final appearance.

28 | Center Star Medallion

WOOD MEDALLION inlays on a floor are beautiful, but the real thing is pretty costly. With this demonstration you can achieve a believable look for a fraction of the cost and you get to entirely customize your medallion.

If you are at a loss for a motif, simply search "hardwood floor inlays" on the Internet and you will find many lovely examples or make up your own!

Entrance halls, libraries, and sun porches can all benefit from this technique.

Remember that you are painting on a floor, so it is best to use floor paints and polyurethanes made especially for floors.

There is no need to apply a topcoat to your entire floor but rather you may simply apply a fresh topcoat to your new beautiful hand-painted medallion. I caution you, neatness counts with this one.

Yes, this medallion is a circle and yes, you can paint a circle if you just remember to breathe. If you really do not want to try to paint a circle, change it to a square.

MATERIALS AND TOOLS

- large adjustable compass
- sandpaper, 220-grit
- latex bonding primer, tinted dark gray
- high-quality angle-edged acrylic artist paintbrush, ¼" (6 mm)
- flat latex floor paint, black
- clear ruler, 2" (5 cm)
- white pencil
- painter's tape
- angle-edged latex paintbrush appropriate for medallion size
- metallic latex paint, brass-colored
- oval sash paintbrush, 2" (5 cm)
- stencil of alphabet
- small stencil brush
- water-based floor polyurethane

1 Determine the placement and size of your star and the background circle. It is best to make a drawing first and lay it on the floor to see if any adjustments are needed.

2 With a compass large enough to make your circle, draw in the circle directly on the floor.

3 Make sure the floor surface you are painting is clean and free of any wax. You may want to sand lightly with 220-grit sandpaper. Apply the dark gray-tinted primer. With the ¼" (6 mm) artist acrylic paintbrush, paint in the outline of your circle. If you are very comfortable with a larger brush, please feel free to use one. Taping a circle never looks good; take your time and you will be able to paint the outline.

4 Once the primer is dry, repeat step 3 with the black floor paint.

5 Draw in the star. The star pattern is made up of two 4-cornered stars with the smaller one drawn in first.

6 Tape off the outline of the star and pounce on the latex metallic paint.

7 When the brass metallic paint is dry, stencil in the compass points and add the smaller black circle to center of star.

8 When all paint is dry, apply water-based floor polyurethane to just your design. You can apply to just the letters using a small brush.

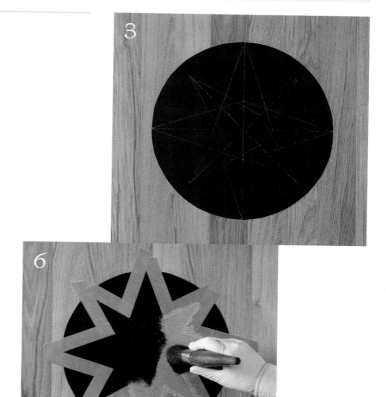

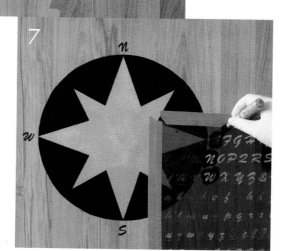

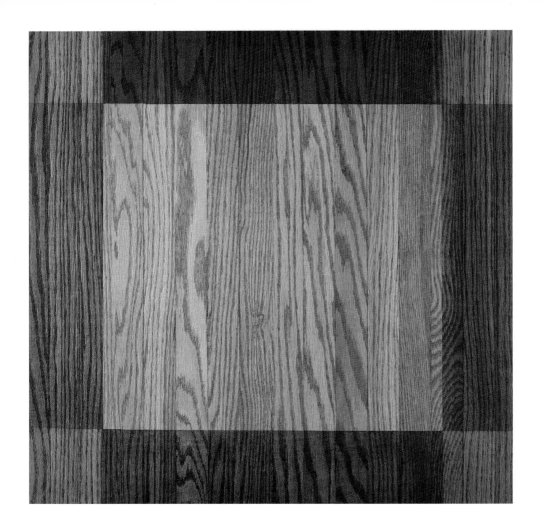

29 Colored Japan Inlay

THE JAPAN paint color Prussian Blue was used in the following demonstration because of the color's beauty and intensity.

Japan paints may be used either as a stain on an unfinished wood floor surface or as a slightly translucent paint over a sealed wood floor surface.

Never overlook the opportunity to use Japan paints as a stain because the colors are so extraordinarily intense and beautiful. This demonstration outlines the Japan paint over an unsealed wood floor surface to create a lovely and soft-colored border and, utilizing the potential of an oil-based paint, simply wiping out more of the paint to create a soft square.

The Japan paint is applied much like a stain. It is thinned down with mineral spirits to a skim-milk consistency and brushed on and wiped off.

If you are applying over a sealed wood floor, do not wipe out the paint, but instead softly brush the color on, blend to eliminate brushstrokes, and then topcoat with an oil-based polyurethane when dry.

Japan paints may be found at good woodworker's stores and online.

MATERIALS AND TOOLS

- painter's tape, 2" (5.1 cm)
- Japan oil paint, Prussian Blue
- flat oil paintbrush, 3" (7.6 cm)
- lint-free rag
- mineral spirits

1 Lay out your border design.

2 With mineral spirits, thin the Japan paint slightly to a skim-milk consistency and brush on, making sure to get into all the cracks.

3 Before the paint is dry, tape off the square made at the border's corners and wipe off yet more of the paint with a rag slightly dampened with mineral spirits.

Do not let the paint dry too long. It's best to do the corner squares as soon as you have applied the two sides.

This will create a soft inset square without any fuss and muss.

30 | Distressed Fir Floor

ARGUABLY fir is not the loveliest of wood grains, so obliterate it! The good news is that fir is very soft so you can distress it with a minimum of effort.

I have even seen where a home-owner had a fir floor installed in a kitchen very early on in the construction process and she wanted the raw fir left uncovered so that all the workers and activity would purposefully mar and distress the floor. When all the work was done, the floor was stained a very dark stain and the result was that she had a floor that looked like it had been there forever.

Pine is also a soft wood that can be distressed easily.

Marring and distressing a floor gives it a worn warmth. If you like this distressing and aged look, read on!

MATERIALS AND TOOLS

- gel stain, Red Mahogany
- gel stain, Dark Walnut
- mineral spirits
- flat oil paintbrush, 3" (7.6 cm)
- hammer
- wood chisel
- nail
- lint-free rag
- satin oil-based floor polyurethane

1 Very lightly stain the floor with a thinned-down gel stain and mineral spirit mixture, 1 to 1.

    This will allow you to see your distressing.

    You do not have to let it completely dry before you begin.

2 Distress the floor. Use a hammer to scratch and dent the surface.

    Use a wood chisel to gouge out areas along the joints.

    Pound a nail in to create holes. Use the nail to scratch and mar the surface.

    Have fun.

3 Apply the mahogany and walnut stains together with the paintbrush and leave on pretty heavy. Use the brush more than a rag to blend and distribute the gel stain.

    Wipe very little stain off with a rag.

    If the first stain coat is not dark enough, apply a second stain coat when the first coat has dried.

    When the stain has dried, seal the surface with a coat or two of satin oil polyurethane.

Note: Always dispose of staining rags according to instructions found on label of stain can—never leave them in the sun or sitting out.

Note: Every day the market improves the water-based stains and dyes, so if you do not want to use oil-based products, try water-based products.

31 | Decking Multi Paints

INSTEAD OF just a solid coating of exterior deck paint, try using more than one color to create interest.

It is not that much more difficult to apply the paint as outlined in the following demonstration and it does allow for some of the grain to show through and will give a softer looking finish to your deck.

This demonstration would also work for the semitransparent stains that you may now find in any good paint store. Follow the same steps if you use the semi-transparent stains.

The following demonstration outlines the use of an exterior deck and floor paint.

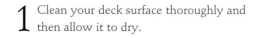
- latex deck paint, warm gray
- flat latex paintbrush, 4" (10.2 cm)
- latex deck paint, white
- lint-free rag

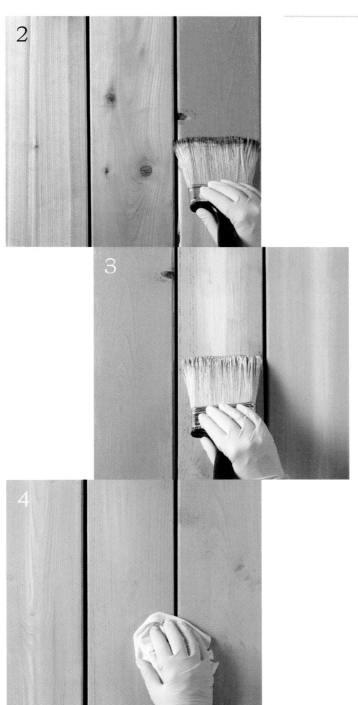

1 Clean your deck surface thoroughly and then allow it to dry.

2 With the paintbrush, brush on some of the warm gray paint.

3 While the gray paint is still wet, apply the white paint next to and into the gray paint with the paintbrush.

4 While all paint is wet, softly pull a lint-free rag through the paint. This will further blend the two colors together and remove some of the paint, revealing some of the wood underneath.

Tip: All paints must be wet before you rag off any, so work in an area comfortable to manipulate and always work end to end to avoid stops and starts in the middle.

Deck paints are fairly "loose" to start with, but you may add a bit of water to your brush to keep the paint a little "looser." Do not add too much water.

32 | Decking Semitransparent Stains

THERE REALLY ARE some wonderful new semitransparent colored stains coming onto the market these days. No longer are we all limited to the standard wood tones.

The exterior areas of homes are now being paid attention to like never before and the public has asked for the same color versatility outside as they have inside. Luckily the manufacturers have responded.

Exterior spaces are now becoming "outside rooms" with all the attention to detail the interiors have enjoyed all these years.

Which means—don't be afraid of color!

The nice thing about the semitransparent stains is that they are just that—stains. A stain will penetrate the wood as opposed to a paint that will sit more on top of the wood surface.

MATERIALS AND TOOLS

- inexpensive flat oil paintbrush, 4" (10.2 cm)
- semitransparent stain, blue
- lint-free rag

1 Make sure the deck surface is clean and completely dry.

2 With the paintbrush, apply the blue stain. If you like the darker blue version as seen in photo 2b, apply a second coat of the stain once the first one has dried completely.

3 Softly wipe stain off with a lint-free rag to remove excess stain. This evens out the stain and distributes the material evenly.

Note: If you use an oil-based semitransparent stain, always dispose of staining rags according to the manufacturer's instructions—do not let the rags sit out!

33 | Faux Bois Repair

WOOD IS ALWAYS all about the color! To have wood graining say wood, it is primarily the color that speaks the loudest and most convincingly. Match the color, add a bit of graining, and you will have a match.

This is a good demonstration to know if you have taken out a wall, have a malfunctioning radiator or a misbehaving pet, and do not want to wait for the repair person to come and patch your floor.

Yes, you could use this technique to cover an entire floor area, in which case just keep going with the instructions outlined here.

- sandpaper, 150-grit (optional)
- latex bonding primer
- UTC, Burnt Umber
- UTC, Raw Umber
- UTC, Raw Sienna
- UTC, Permanent Green
- UTC, Thalo Blue
- flat oil paintbrush, 3" (7.6 cm)
- satin oil-based floor polyurethane
- lint-free rag
- hair dryer (optional)
- painter's tape, 2" (5.1 cm)

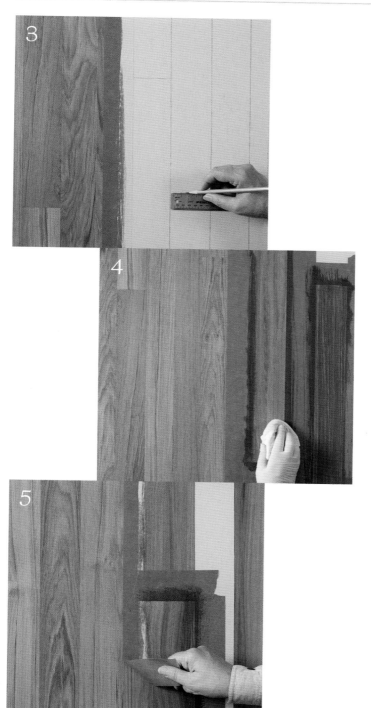

1 Make sure the section you need to repair is clean and dry. You may have to sand it with 150-grit sandpaper first.

2 Tint your primer to the lightest color found in the wood you are matching.

Apply to the section you need to repair.

Keep brushstrokes in the pattern of the existing wood grain.

3 Draw in your new wood planks. Mask off alternating planks to give a look of realism.

The UTC list above is large, but you will find that those are generally the tints that will you get you where you need to go with the basecoat and the graining solution.

Apply two coats of basecoat and allow them each to completely dry.

Have brushstrokes of the basecoat follow the grain pattern.

4 Slowly add UTC drops to satin oil polyurethane, matching the existing wood color. Match the medium/dark coloration.

Brush the woodgrain-tinted polyurethane onto the taped-off exposed "planks."

Take a lint-free rag and gently pull through the graining material a few times to create a grain.

Play with it a bit; you will get a believable grain.

5 You can use a hair dryer to force-dry the oil polyurethane so you may continue. Force-dry until the sheen has dulled down; then you can apply tape without smearing your work and continue until you are finished.

Make sure your tape is securely pressed down.

6 After a 24-hour dry, apply a coat of polyurethane that matches the sheen of the rest of the floor.

34 | Antiqued Brick Pavers

IF YOU WOULD like to change the look of dark red brick (or in this case, dark red brick pavers) to something else altogether, you may do so! You are not stuck with this color if you do not want it and you do not have to go through the expense of removal and putting something new in.

At least try this demonstration as a way to have the color you want before you go ripping everything out.

If you have interior bricks of this nature, follow the same steps to help those along too.

The antiquing of the new color will lend yet another layer of interest and realism to your new pavers.

1 Clean the pavers. The basecoat could be almost solid covering, but doesn't need to be.

   If you use a roller, do not leave roller marks. A brush is easier to control.

2 After the basecoat has completely dried, mix the dark "dirt" color.

   If you have black paint, turn it to "dirt" by adding ¼ of the white paint and a healthy squirt of UTC Burnt Umber with a dash of UTC Raw Umber. You do not want it black but rather "dirty" looking.

   Apply dark paint with the paintbrush.

   Dip brush into water, then into paint, and then onto surface.

3 While the dark paint is still wet, remove some with a wet rag.

   Look to see where dirt and age would build up and take your lead from these areas.

   You do not have to cover with the gray basecoat 100%.

   You may leave the dark color on as heavy as you want or remove as much as you want.

   You may thin the dark paint down with water if you want a less dramatic look.

   Just be sure that you do not let the dark paint dry out before you have had a chance to remove.

   Work in an area that you can comfortably reach and blend the wet paint into dried paint carefully.

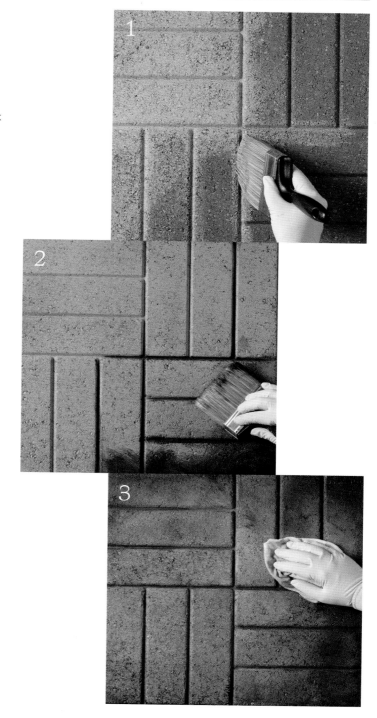

35 Freshened Sheet Vinyl B&W Squares

SICK OF YOUR same old vinyl? Don't want to replace it, but want something more interesting? You can paint it with this simple yet effective technique.

This demonstration will show you how you can freshen up what is probably a perfectly good vinyl floor that you are just a little tired of.

Always try to make your job easier for yourself by not doing the whole area but just punching the floor up in selected areas with selected colors. You can sit on your floor, relaxed, and have fun transforming what is old into what is new.

Remember to always strip off any wax buildup and dirt before applying any paint.

1 Decide which squares you want to paint.

2 Prime with white latex bonding primer the squares you want white.

Prime with dark latex bonding primer the squares you want black.

You will notice that the embossing on the surface of the linoleum is not straight, so you do not even need to paint a straight line.

Simply hold the brush flat to the surface and follow the embossed edge around the squares and try not to get a paint ridge along the edges. Holding your brush flat to the surface will help with this.

3 After drying, apply the white semigloss latex paint to the primed white squares.

Do the same with the black semigloss painted over the darker primed squares.

4 To protect your paint, apply a coat or two of semigloss floor polyurethane to the squares that have been painted.

36 | Awning Stripes

REMEMBER THE OLD flecked vinyl tile floors that maybe you had in your bedroom or playroom as a child, the floors that were popular because they are easy to install and wear amazingly well? Unfortunately, these vinyl tiles did not come in any impressive array of colors.

It is always a pity to have to replace a perfectly good vinyl floor when it is in good condition, securely adhered, or otherwise in perfectly good shape and has served you well.

Maybe you do not have to replace it—just yet.

This demonstration will show how you can spiff up that tired yet still serviceable vinyl floor.

Stripes are fun and easy to paint and will give your room a sense of casualness.

Render in a muted color palette for a more sophisticated appearance or have a bit of fun with color, as this demonstration shows.

Take your inspiration from an awning perhaps seen out of a window or even your favorite striped bedding.

Exaggerate the size of the stripe and you will add visual space and direction to the room.

MATERIALS AND TOOLS

- painter's tape
- flat latex paintbrushes appropriate to size
- foam roller brush (optional)
- latex bonding primer
- flat latex paint, color of your choice
- latex floor polyurethane, sheen of your choice

1 Completely clean any and all wax and dirt off the floor. Use a wax stripper if need be. The floor surface must be clean.

2 Use the tape to create the stripes. You can lay out your design before you begin or you can just begin to put in the stripe.

Use the areas under the tape to reveal the original floor and become a stripe. Because of this, tape should always be laid down straight, keeping in mind what is underneath is also a stripe.

3 Burnish the tape edges down very well. With a brush or roller, apply a coat of primer to the exposed stripes.

Note: It is easier if you allow some of the blue tape to show, as this will help you see where the stripes are if you have taped off a large area.

4 Apply your colors. Stripe should be opaque, so depending upon your color(s) apply one or two coats after first coat is completely dry.

5 Pull the tape as soon as you can and always pull tape at a 45° angle away from the painted surface. Apply 2 coats of latex polyurethane in the sheen of your choice.

37 | Arcs & Circles

THIS DEMONSTRATION is about the imagery more than what you put it on. These arcs and circles would look beautiful over just about any floor surface. Always remember to use compatible paints with the right surface.

Imagine very soft Japan paints over a previously sealed hardwood floor.

Instead of solidly painting the arcs and circles, you could use stains on a raw wood floor, creating softly colored shapes.

Feel free to make the arcs and circles as big or small as you want. You will have fun drawing in your patterns—just remember that less is probably more and don't get lost!

- string
- pencil
- latex enamel floor paint
- angle-edged artist acrylic paintbrush, ½" (1.3 cm)
- angle-edged latex paintbrush, 3" (7.6 cm)
- latex floor polyurethane (optional)

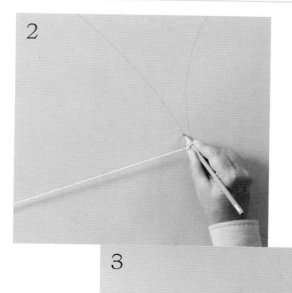

1 Tie an arm's length of string around a pencil. To make an arc, hold one end of the string down tightly to the floor, extend your arm and hand until the string is very tight, and making sure the hand that is holding down the string does not let the string go loose, place the pencil to the floor and draw from side to side, always keeping tension on the string—voilà—a perfect arc!

It is that simple. You can do even larger arcs if you have someone else hold the other end.

2 Continue with step 1 and remember to turn your body now and then to change arc direction.

To make circles, simply have someone hold one end while you move around with the pencil or make smaller ones you can complete.

3 When outlines are complete, begin to paint in the inside angle portions first.

Use the smaller paintbrush to paint in the outline; then use the larger paintbrush to fill in.

It is always easier to follow an outside curve with a paintbrush as opposed to an inside angle.

Use the smaller angle-edged brush to fit into the tight angles.

4 Paint in the outside curved shapes.

5 Keep going until you are done. You may want to topcoat your work of art with the appropriate polyurethane.

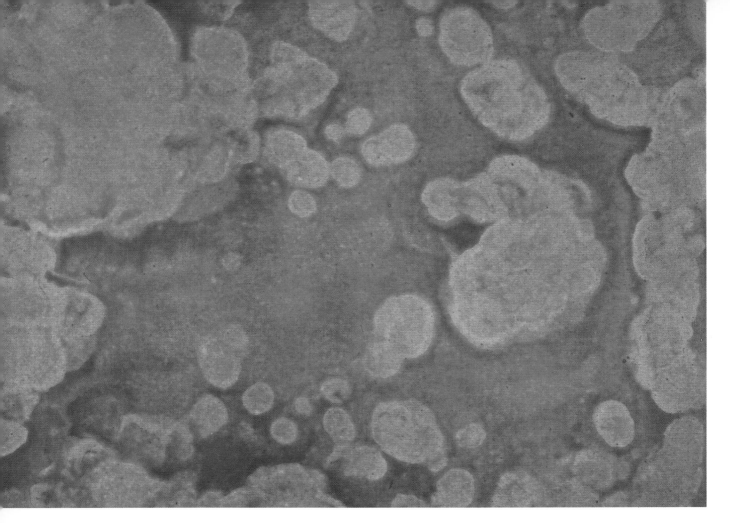

38 | Faux Cement Stain

DO YOU HAVE a cement floor somewhere in your house that you would like to have look more interesting? If you have seen the cement stains available on today's market, you know the beauty that can be achieved on a plain old cement floor. However, the cement floor in your home is perhaps already painted or sealed, which means you cannot apply one of these lovely cement stains, as they go either into wet or onto unsealed cement.

Good news! You can achieve a very similar look by merely tinting a floor topcoat.

This demonstration is for water-based floor polyurethane only, which can be applied over previously painted latex floor paint or a yet unpainted but sealed cement floor.

If the technique looks too difficult for a large floor, always remember that you can mask off the floor into manageable sections. The larger, the better, but work an area you are comfortable with. You should not start and stop this finish in the middle of an area.

Generally the cement stains tend to be earth-tone colors of warm browns and greens and that is why these colors have been selected for this demonstration.

MATERIALS AND TOOLS

- UTC, Burnt Umber
- water-based satin floor polyurethane
- gloves
- UTC, Yellow
- UTC, Permanent Green
- flat latex paintbrush, 4" (10.2 cm)
- denatured alcohol
- UTC, Black

1 Mix UTC Burnt Umber into the polyurethane. Mix UTC Yellow and Permanent Green together in another container of polyurethane in equal amounts.

Please read page 16 on mixing UTC.

2 With your brush and working in small sections, French brush (page 16) the two tinted polyurethanes together. Do not add water to your poly; rather dip your brush into water every third load or so. You want the poly to remain wet and rather soupy on the floor.

3 Before polyurethane begins to set up and while it is still very wet, dip your hand in denatured alcohol and let some drop off your fingers. Stay close to the floor surface; this will allow larger "puddles" to form. The application of the alcohol will break up any brushstrokes, ooze the colors together, and add an interesting element.

Allow to dry completely.

4 After you have applied the two colors of poly and the alcohol to the entire surface and it has dried completely, maybe even overnight, you will now apply a coat of the same two polyurethane colors with the addition of a third: black-tinted poly.

Apply quickly in the French brush manner. You may use the same brush and you may dip the brush into water every now and then to keep brushstrokes down.

Do not over-brush the poly and it will level out better.

You want this coat to bury the previous work and cut down the contrast of the light areas.

You may have to repeat this step to further bury and reduce contrast once the previous coat of poly is dry.

Tip: Have someone help you by applying the alcohol as you apply the poly.

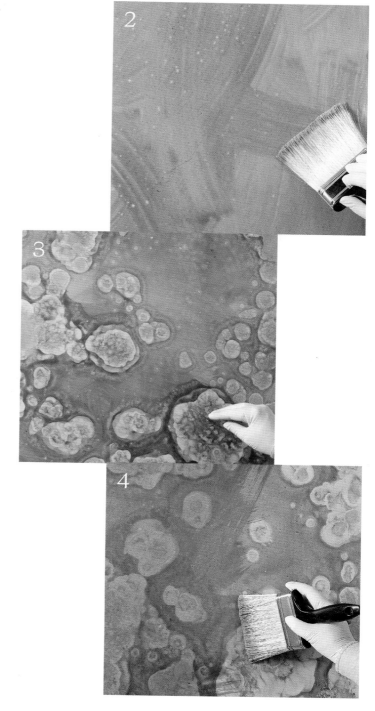

39 French Ironwork Stencil

A BEAUTIFUL WAY to treat a large unbroken slab of cement flooring (or any other type of flooring for that matter) is with a general overall pattern. The pattern chosen for this demonstration is that of French ironwork because the delicacy of the pattern plays out over a large surface in a lovely way. Light and airy in design, yet due to the receptiveness, substantial and interesting underfoot.

No need for a throw rug here.

As with any stencil, always use the same side and directional orientation throughout your application and always remember to put in the registration marks!

- chalk line
- triangle
- large floor stencil
- foam roller brush, 4" (10.2 cm)
- latex enamel floor paint, dark gray
- hair dryer

1 Determine the middle of the floor using a chalk line.

Have someone hold the line in one corner while you pull it out to the diagonally opposite corner. Pull the line taut and snap it against the floor. Repeat for the other corners. Where the two lines intersect is your center.

To be sure you are going straight (or level), use a triangle and make a square from the diagonals. You are now centered and true.

This is important because all the other stencils will come off of this very first one.

Line stencil up on center.

2 Load the roller with the paint and, moving from center out, roll over the stencil.

You may wish to use a temporary fix-it spray on the back of the stencil to hold it in position, but as it is on the floor, usually just one or two pieces of tape will hold the stencil in place.

3 Force the paint dry with the hair dryer if it is not already and match up the registration marks and continue as you did in step 2 until the area is complete.

Note: If you are applying the stencil over a painted cement floor, there is no need to apply a topcoat, as you are using the same type of floor paint. Be careful with the fresh stencil floor paint for at least a week while the paint cures.

If you are applying the stencil over unpainted (raw) cement, talk to your paint store clerk to see if you would need to apply a cement sealer first.

If your raw cement floor is not damp and has no moisture problem and if you use a good cement floor paint, you should not need to seal the entire floor first, but ask.

40 Cement to Stone

THIS IS AN amazingly versatile technique. The material you will be using has many different surface applications, from exterior pavers to interior linoleum.

You may now find in your local paint stores this spreading stone material. If your paint store doesn't carry this product, you can find it online; search for "spreadable stone."

Keep in mind that you will want to follow the manufacturer's instructions and use all their products found in the system, even the grout tape, to ensure a compatible result. I have found the spreading stone systems to be all quite good and they are products of high quality.

This is a demonstration of how you can make a regular old interior cement floor look like a beautiful stone floor in a very easy manner.

A white spreading stone material was used because the material can be color washed with water mixed with powder dyes provided by the manufacturer. The look and manipulation of these dyes gives a more believable stone finish.

This finish has texture, which also lends itself to a true stone look.

Dark gray floor paint was used as the basecoat color, which will show through in random places, becoming part of the stone finish.

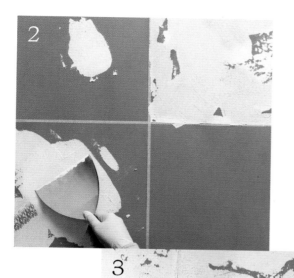

1 Determine your pattern. Apply the grout line tape provided by manufacturer. Do not substitute regular ¼" (6 mm) tape, as the manufacturer's has a fiber content that allows you to be able to remove it.

2 Place a small amount of spreading stone onto a section. You do not want the depth of the material to exceed 1/16" (1.6 mm).

Using your spreading blade, pull the material in a 45° angle to the right angles of your section. Be a bit rough with the material; gouge out areas and softly blade over to create pits. Have some of the gray basecoat color peek through. Think of a stone surface.

3 Continue applying the spreading stone until all your areas are covered. The material will set up fairly quickly.

4 Once you have applied the spreading stone material to all of your surface areas and it has dried, pull the grout tape off.

With the spreading blade, softly burnish over the surface to remove any burrs or little chunks.

Mix the powder dyes with water according to the manufacturer's instructions.

Rag on the two colors of golden brown and darker brown.

Blend together to remove rag marks. Allow to dry a bit, and then with a water-dampened rag remove some of the color from the high parts while leaving color to remain in the crevices.

Tip: If you are doing a large surface in this fashion you do not need to do each "stone" individually. You may cover more than one 12" x 12" (30.5 x 30.5 cm) section at a time. Change direction every now and then to create a realistic result—just like Mother Nature.

41 | Bluestone with Brick

TIRED OF THE concrete or cement patio slab? Think concrete or cement can't be painted? Oh, it can. Ask at the paint store for a paint that will go on concrete or cement and tell them if it is for exterior or interior application. There are paints that are for masonry, cement, and concrete and they are water-based. So the sky is the limit when plotting your new patio.

Tell the clerk that you are painting a concrete or cement floor and he or she will guide you to the right sealers and paints.

The most important part is that your concrete or cement is very clean and very dry before you begin any applications.

If you get a bit of wear in your artwork you can either fix it or let the wear become part of the overall look.

Be brave and have fun turning the slab into something beautiful.

- latex paint suitable for concrete, dark gray
- medium value latex paint suitable for concrete, beige

- latex paint suitable for concrete, black
- latex paint suitable for concrete, brick red
- painter's tape

- flat latex paintbrush, 3" (7.6 cm)
- lint-free rag
- pail of water

1 Lay out your design.

2 Tape off what will be your grout lines and begin to apply paint to create the bluestone.

Dip the 3" (7.6 cm) brush into dark gray paint generously and paint in a couple of "rows."

Before the dark gray paint is dry, dip the same brush into the beige paint and apply paint next to and over the dark gray, blending the two together some.

To create texture, turn the brush sideways and pounce some of the paints together.

While all paints are still wet, stroke the paintbrush over the surface, blending and softening even further.

You could just tip your paintbrush into water to help with the blending.

The key is to keep all the paints wet so that you may soften and blend the colors together.

3 Continue until all bluestone is complete. Notice that the direction alters for the different pieces.

4 Paint in the brick. Pounce some black paint on. Pounce some brick red paint on and over and next to the black.

Blend the two colors.

While paint is wet, texture with a rag.

Continue to use the rag to soften out the texture a bit.

Tip: Work only in an area you can reach at one time so you can keep the paints wet. The bluestone has a soft striation as its grain, so change the direction of the pieces for more interest.

42 | Venetian Pavers

TIRED OF YOUR existing pavers? Want to add some pizzazz or fun surprises? You can change the color of pavers.

This demonstration uses a "Venetian color palette," the brightly colored blues, reds, and yellows that you will find underfoot as you stroll through Venice. However, as is always the case, feel free to create your own palette!

Always use exterior paints if your pavers are outside and discuss with your paint salesperson the best paint to use for masonry. Remember, you can change the colors and make up colors by using your UTCs.

You will be applying and removing the paint, so if over time your painted areas show wear, relax and appreciate the natural wear and tear. The paint is supposed to look a bit old and worn!

MATERIALS AND TOOLS

- exterior latex masonry paint
- angle-edged latex paintbrush, 2" (5.1 cm)
- UTCs (optional) to alter color
- lint-free rag

1 Decide your pattern.

2 Apply your first color. Simply brush on, but do not get too far ahead of yourself, as you want to keep the paint wet to be able to rag off some.

 If the paint seems too thick, or if you are in the sun and the paint is drying too quickly, dip your brush in water every other time before you load the brush with paint.

3 Before yellow paint has dried, water-wash the yellow paint by dipping brush into water and wash over the applied yellow paint.

 Immediately take a lint-free rag and rag off as much paint as you desire.

4 Continue the above steps—and sequence of paint, water, and rag—with your other colors until complete.

Tip: Do not dilute the paint too much with water, as this will weaken it. Instead try to apply it full-bodied and use a little water to just help rag off some paint.

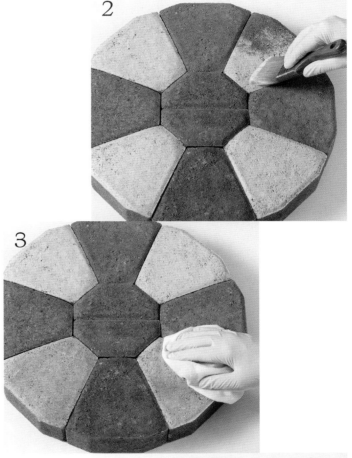

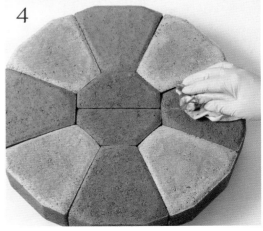

And So Much M O R E

43 | Faux Bois Door

THIS TECHNIQUE IS wonderful for that fire door between your kitchen and garage or just anytime you might want to add a wood-grained door or match a door to existing woodwork found in a room.

If your woodwork is painted and you have a beautiful raised paneled door that is also painted, no need to go through the mess and fuss of stripping—merely wood-grain the door! A wood door set into painted frames and within a room where the woodwork has been painted are absolutely acceptable in terms of good design.

Actually quite a traditional approach was to highlight the beautiful wood of the door by leaving that the only element not painted.

Remember, you may choose any color for your door, deepen the color, and add a bit of antiquing to the wood graining once it has dried for a rich look. Or, you can lighten the wood graining once it has dried with a white color wash for a contemporary look.

Please read the demonstration for Faux Bois Repair (page 88), as the information will be helpful.

MATERIALS AND TOOLS

- latex bonding primer
- eggshell latex paint for basecoat
- flat natural chip paintbrush, 3" (7.6 cm)
- UTC, Burnt Umber
- UTC, Raw Umber

- UTC, Raw Sienna
- lint-free rag
- flogger brush
- satin oil-based varnish
- mineral spirits

- painter's tape, 1" (2.5 cm)
- hair dryer (optional)
- flat natural chip paintbrush, 1" (2.5 cm)
- sandpaper, 80-grit

1 Primer and basecoat the door to be wood-grained. If you are matching existing wood, the basecoat should match the lightest color found in the wood you are matching.

Use a white, eggshell-sheen paint and color it with your UTCs if you do not want to buy a quart of paint.

2 Mix the desired wood-graining glaze by adding UTC colorant to satin oil varnish to achieve the desired color. If the varnish is too "sticky," you may add a small amount of mineral spirits to loosen the varnish up.

3 Apply the wood-graining glaze with a chip brush to the interior panels first.

4 Softly wipe through the glaze with a lint-free rag to create a wood pattern. Leave the recessed panel portion less textured.

5 With your flogger brush, start at the top of the panel and lightly flog downward. The pressure is light and the brush should be held almost parallel to the door surface.

Try not to hit the completed raised panel portion.

With a rag dampened with a bit of mineral spirits, wipe off excess glaze from around the panel.

6 Repeat steps 3, 4, and 5 along the rails doing one section at a time.

You may lightly tape over a glazed section (to get a nice crisp edge) once the varnish has dulled down. You may use a hair dryer to force-dry the varnish if you need to. Do not get fresh varnish on previously varnished surface.

44 Faux Stainless Steel

HAVE A PERFECTLY good refrigerator, large or small, that no longer matches your décor? You do not have to look at it and not like it—paint it!

Great for wet bars, dorm rooms, or even the kitchen refrigerator.

Choose a latex-based metallic paint close to the color of your existing stainless. You may add a few drops of UTC to tweak the color if you need to. Or you might find that a warm champagne metallic mixed with a silver metallic will match the coloration.

Obviously this finish does not go well over the pebbly textured appliance fronts. But it does work well over flat fronts.

Dishwashers and trash compactors both can benefit from this technique.

You will want to prime the surface to be painted with a high-quality latex bonding primer tinted to a color close to your metallic color. The primer should be painted in the same fashion as described below for the metallic.

The reason being: stainless has a slight grain in it and you want to simulate that grain, so a slight linear pattern to your brushwork is desirable.

MATERIALS AND TOOLS

- high-quality latex bonding primer, tinted to a color close to metallic color
- metallic latex paint
- flat latex paintbrush, 3" (7.6 cm) or 4" (10.2 cm)
- metal straightedge
- satin latex polyurethane

1 Prime your surface and allow to completely dry.

2 Apply the metallic paint in a very straight up-and-down manner with the paintbrush. To keep your strokes straight, place a straightedge onto the surface and use as a guide for your brush.

3 After the first coat of metallic paint has completely dried, apply a second coat in the same manner.

4 Clearcoat your artwork with durable latex polyurethane.

Frosted Mirror

DO YOU HAVE a wall of mirrors that you want to freshen up? The use of an interesting stencil pattern and a can of "frosted glass" can add interest and a pattern to a room.

This pattern will bring a soft contemporary feel to any mirror.

This demonstration shows an overall coverage, but certainly feel free to mask off and apply as a border only if you so wish.

Make your job easier by using a simple design stencil. A larger and more simplistic design works best. The "frosted glass" used here was created with a spray can, which is an effective and easy application for simple designs.

Because you are working on a glass surface you should not use a low-tack stencil adhesive to keep in place, as it will transfer to the surface. A larger stencil is heavier and will lie flatter.

If you get tired of the look or wish to fix a mistake, simply scrape off with a safety razor, being careful not to scratch the glass, and wipe clean with some denatured alcohol.

Use the aerosol-frosted glass in a well-ventilated area and always follow the manufacturer's instructions.

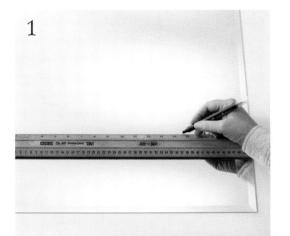

1 Before starting anything, make sure that your surface is clean and dry.

It is important to have the first stencil centered and straight, as you will be working from the stencil register marks after the first stencil is made.

Start in the middle of the wall, lining up the stencil on the centerline. Bubble rulers have a level on them and are very handy for keeping your work level.

2 Mark the face of the stencil with a piece of tape indicating the top.

Position the first stencil directly over the centerline and tape into place at the top corners.

Use the white paper to mask off all surrounding areas against overspray. Apply masking paper to the stencil, not the mirrored surface. You may keep this paper attached if it is not in your way.

Keeping one hand on the bottom of the stencil, spray on the frosted glass material. Use gloves because the frosted glass will get on your hands.

Spray the material in short bursts; do not apply heavily. Less is better.

Make sure to mark register marks with black water-based marker.

3 You may proceed horizontally or vertically, whichever you would prefer. Always make sure that the face of the stencil is toward you.

Always make sure your register marks are lined up.

Always make sure you have masked the surrounding area against overspray.

Continue until all the surface area is covered.

Allow to dry overnight and the next day you may clean up any mistakes or overspray carefully with a safety razor.

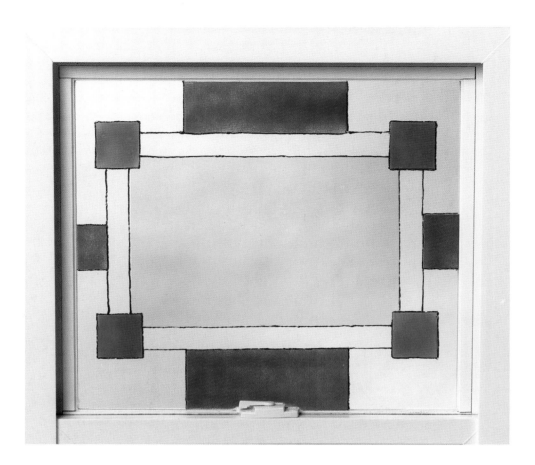

46 Imitation Stained Glass

THIS DEMONSTRATION OUTLINES how to make any window look like a stained glass window. Use it to jazz up the boring sidelight windows to doors, or add something fun to your child's windows.

For those of us who do not know how to construct stained glass, this is an easy alternative and a versatile look to our windows.

If you get tired of the look, the paints and faux leading may be removed with a safety razor and/or lacquer thinner.

Follow a monochromatic color palette for a sophisticated look or add color and whimsy to any environment with this fun application.

There are many stained glass pattern books on the market from arts-and-crafts style to free form. Search and execute!

MATERIALS AND TOOLS

- white paper
- clear plastic ruler, 2" (5.1 cm)
- felt-tip marker
- Spray Stained Glass (found in crafts stores)
- painter's tape, 6" (15.2 cm)
- handheld masking machine
- blue painter's tape
- liquid leading

1 Lay out your pattern on a piece of paper first and when you are satisfied, transfer the pattern to the window by placing the drawn layout behind the glass surface you will be painting.

Using your marker, draw the pattern onto front of glass.

Mask off the area you will be spraying with the Spray Glass and apply in short sweeping motions. Make sure all surrounding areas are masked off and protected from the Spray Glass.

Do not spray too heavily, as the paint will run.

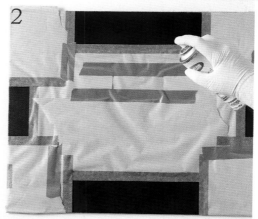

2 Repeat the masking and spraying of the red and blue Spray Glass colors, allowing the dry time suggestions found on the label.

3 When all the colors have been applied and dried, apply the liquid leading material following the lines you made with your marker.

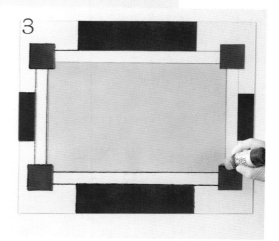

Note: You may do more intricate patterns if your glass is not installed. Simply find a pattern and set it underneath a piece of glass, sort of like a "paint by number." There are also stained glass paints that come in a liquid form which are better for the more intricate designs that you can do with your glass flat in front of you.

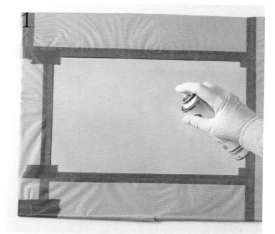

47 | Antiqued Crown Molding

THE QUESTION IS always: is the crown molding part of the wall or part of the ceiling? If the crown moldings are incorporated into the ceiling, you get a lovely "cap" or "lid" to your walls, so please, experiment with making the crown molding part of the ceiling.

The finish described here is a standard and easy antiquing demonstration. In fact, it's so easy that you may want to continue it onto all the painted woodwork in the room for a truly special look.

Soft and subtle, the slight antiquing gives interest and shading to white woodwork and softens the contrast between walls and ceilings.

The demonstration shows latex antiquing glaze over latex enamel. However, if your woodwork is painted in an oil enamel, please use an oil paint for the antiquing glaze mixed the same proportions, but use alkyl glazing liquid, instead of water-based glazing liquid, and mineral spirits instead of water.

1 Mix the antiquing glaze: 1 part paint, 1 part glazing liquid, and 1 part water.

2 Brush the antiquing glaze into the recesses of the molding.

3 Load the brush with the glaze and draw over the entire surface with just one continuous stroke.

4 Immediately take a soft lint-free rag and with one stroke remove some of the glaze from the high points of the molding, leaving a heavier deposit in the low points. The trick is to keep working before the paint dries out, but you should have plenty of time. If you remove too much from certain areas, continue around the room; then go back and gently touch up.

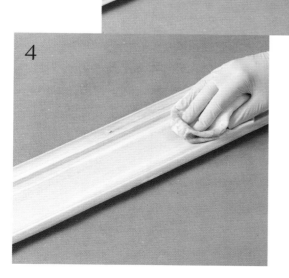

48 | Aged Molding

WHEN YOU WANT the look of aged and darkening varnish, this simple technique works well and is very easy.

A beautiful baseboard complement to a distressed floor, the molding will enhance the richness of the floor and create a unified design element within the room.

The technique is purposefully done to appear old and dark. It's a beautiful way to have a dark colored molding without having to paint it.

We are all accustomed to seeing light-colored moldings in a room, but for a dramatic change try going to the dark side—the result can be quite stunning and handsome.

This treatment will warm a room up and speak of a long life.

No glaze is mixed in this demonstration because the black paint is used full-bodied.

This finish is for use on raw wood.

MATERIALS AND TOOLS

- gel stain, Golden Oak
- lint-free rags
- gel stain, Dark Walnut
- semigloss latex paint, black
- angle-edged latex paintbrush, 2" (5.1 cm)

1 Apply the Golden Oak gel stain to 100% of the surface with a lint-free rag.

2 Immediately apply the Dark Walnut gel stain with a lint-free rag, not all over but rather selectively, into the crevices and along the edges, pulling some onto the flat face portion of the board and blend together with the Golden Oak.

Work the two stains together with a lint-free rag.

Allow the gel stains to dry, following the label instructions.

3 Apply the black paint thinly into the recesses and along the edges and some of the face.

Immediately wipe with a soft water-dampened rag to remove, blend into, and soften the black paint.

If the paint feels too thick, dip your brush in a bit of water—not too much, just a tip.

Do not apply too much black paint; you want to be able to pull the black paint out onto the surface and remove.

Tip: Work quickly so that the black paint remains wet and able to be removed and blended.

Remember that if the black latex paint dries out on you, denatured alcohol on a rag will remove it.

Note: The rags from the gel stains are flammable; follow manufacturer's label instructions on proper disposal. Do NOT leave the rags lying out after use.

49 | Metallic Tiles

HAVE YOU EVER tried to dig out just a few tiles? Not very easy… Want to add a bit of something new to your tile walls?

Metallic tiles are quite popular now and are not cheap, so this demonstration will show you how you can simply paint your own right onto your existing tiles.

Consider using an existing pat-tern that also might be in the room. Couple the metallic look with a frosted mirror (page 114) or comple-ment a stained glass window that you have made for the window (page 116). Or simply randomly decide to make certain tiles metallic. No need to limit yourself to just one metallic color—consider copper and gold and aluminum!

1 Mask off the surrounding tiles from the ones you want to apply the metallic paint to.

Run the tape just along the edge of the grout where it meets the tile.

Make sure everything around the area to be sprayed is well masked.

Spray the primer on.

2 Immediately remove all tape and masking paper. When primer is dry, re-tape the tiles that are to receive the metallic paint.

Cut a small 2" x 2" (5.1 x 5.1 cm) piece of sponge from a larger wallpaper sponge.

Apply the metallic paint to the primed tiles with the sponge.

Dab the paint straight up and down until you have eliminated the air bubbles.

Immediately pull the tape before the metallic paint dries; otherwise the tape will most likely pull the dried metallic paint off along the edges.

50 Reverse Color Molding

PEOPLE ALWAYS PAINT their moldings white—why not do the opposite and paint them black? A black molding is a dramatic molding and really is a lovely touch to any color scheme. Black, just like white, goes with anything—it is merely the opposite end of the spectrum.

To further add a touch of intrigue and mystery to the color black, this demonstration will show you how a few extra steps will really make the black molding a special and sophisticated element.

While this demonstration shows the high contrast of beige against black in the early stages, if you like the appearance of your molding with just these colors painted on, feel free to consider yourself finished!

You may also use a color other than beige and merely use that color in place of the beige as outlined in the following instructions.

MATERIALS AND TOOLS

- eggshell latex enamel paint, beige
- high-quality angle-edged latex paintbrush, 2" (5.1 cm)
- eggshell latex enamel paint, black
- latex glazing liquid
- water
- lint-free rag

1 The molding has been primed first in a color very close to the beige eggshell enamel paint.

Paint the narrow section of the molding with the beige enamel paint.

2 When the beige paint is dry, paint on the black eggshell enamel paint.

Note: No need to tape, merely cut in the black paint. The line does not have to be perfect—but close.

Also, the black paint does not have to be 100% opaque—but close.

3 When all paint is dry, mix a black glaze (⅓ black paint, ⅓ latex glazing liquid, and ⅓ water) and carefully brush over the beige paint.

Before the paint is dry, wipe with a lint-free rag to lightly antique the beige paint.

If you like the molding at this point, you are done.

4 Once the beige paint has dried, apply beige glaze (⅓ beige paint, ⅓ latex glazing liquid, and ⅓ water) over the black portion of the molding.

Before the beige paint is dry, rag off as much as you want of the beige paint.

Note: When moving from one section to the next, do not apply the glaze right where you left off. Instead start a little ahead and feather the paint back into the previously painted area.

If the glaze seems too "wet," add more paint and glazing liquid in equal amounts to thicken up.

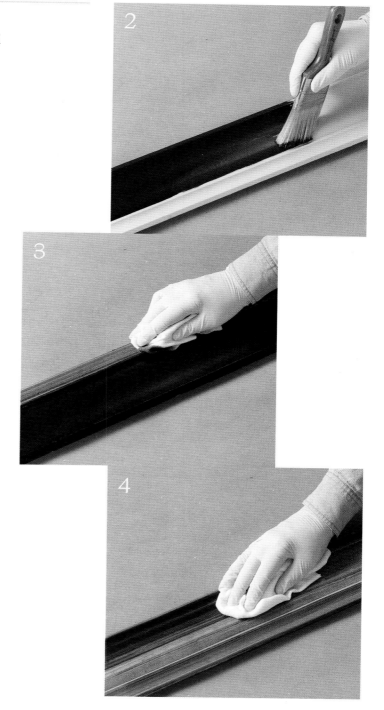

Author Biography

Elise Kinkead is an expert decorative painter specializing in the art of painted finishes for furniture and decoration. She has worked for select clients all over the country and also designs wall coverings. Her work has been published in local, regional, and national magazines. She is the author of *50 Ways to Paint Furniture* and co-author of *Mastering Fine Decorative Paint Techniques.*

Besides loving any surface as a canvas, she enjoys sharing her knowledge with others so that they may realize the delight in creating an object of beauty by challenging their artist within—both for self satisfaction and for the enjoyment of those who view the project.

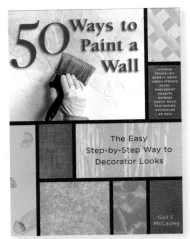

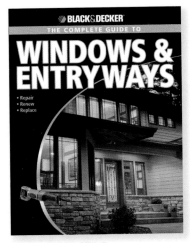